GREALISH

MATT AND TOM OLDFIELD

ULTIMATE
FOOTBALL HEROES

GREALISH

FROM THE PLAYGROUND
TO THE PITCH

DINO

First published by Dino Books in 2021,
an imprint of Bonnier Books UK,
4th Floor, Victoria House, Bloomsbury Square, London WC1B 4DA
Owned by Bonnier Books,
Sveavägen 56, Stockholm, Sweden

@UFHbooks
@footieheroesbks
www.heroesfootball.com
www.bonnierbooks.co.uk

Text © Matt Oldfield 2021
The right of Matt Oldfield to be identified as the author of this work has been
asserted by him in accordance with the Copyright, Designs and Patents Act 1988.

Design by www.envydesign.co.uk

Paperback ISBN: 978 1 78946 476 4
E-book ISBN: 978 1 78946 477 1

British Library cataloguing-in-publication data:
A catalogue record for this book is available from the British Library.

Printed and bound in Great Britain by Clays Ltd, Elcograf S.p.A.

1 3 5 7 9 10 8 6 4 2

Matt Oldfield is an accomplished writer and the editor-in-chief of football review site Of Pitch & Page. Tom Oldfield is a freelance sports writer and the author of biographies on Cristiano Ronaldo, Arsène Wenger and Rafael Nadal.

Cover illustration by Dan Leydon.
To learn more about Dan visit danleydon.com
To purchase his artwork visit etsy.com/shop/footynews
Or just follow him on Twitter @danleydon

TABLE OF CONTENTS

ACKNOWLEDGEMENTS

First of all, I'd like to thank everyone at Bonnier
Books UK for supporting me throughout and for
running the ever-expanding UFH ship so smoothly.
Writing stories for the next generation of football fans
is both an honour and a pleasure. Thanks also to my
agent, Nick Walters, for helping to keep my dream
job going, year after year.

Next up, an extra big cheer for all the teachers,
booksellers and librarians who have championed these
books, and, of course, for the readers. The success
of this series is truly down to you.

Okay, onto friends and family. I wouldn't be writing
this series if it wasn't for my brother Tom. I owe him

so much and I'm very grateful for his belief in me as an author. I'm also very grateful to the rest of my family, especially Mel, Noah, Nico, and of course Mum and Dad. To my parents, I owe my biggest passions: football and books. They're a real inspiration for everything I do.

Pang, Will, Mills, Doug, Naomi, John, Charlie, Sam, Katy, Ben, Karen, Ana (and anyone else I forgot) – thanks for all the love and laughs, but sorry, no I won't be getting 'a real job' anytime soon!

And finally, I couldn't have done any of this without Iona's encouragement and understanding. Much love to you.

CHAPTER 1

ENGLAND'S EURO SUPER SUB

29 June 2021, Wembley Stadium, London

England vs Germany – it was one of the most famous international matches in football. And to add to the tension and excitement surrounding the game, this time the two nations were competing for a place in the Euro 2020 quarter-finals. So, which country would be the winners?

Despite all the passionate singing in the stadium and all the talented players on the pitch, the first half was a tight one, with lots of passing and tackling, but not much shooting. For Germany, Timo Werner missed a one-on-one with Jordan Pickford, and for

England, Harry Kane fluffed a glorious chance in the final seconds.

Half-time score: 0–0.

Everyone at Wembley was hoping for more entertainment in the second half, but as the minutes ticked by, it was Germany who were doing most of the attacking, and England who were doing most of the defending. It was nerve-jangling stuff for the home fans to watch, and whenever the Three Lions did get the ball, they hoofed it forward to Harry and Raheem Sterling, who were all on their own up front.

'Come on, England!' the supporters cheered, but they were losing confidence. Was their Euro 2020 dream about to end? What they needed was a moment of magic, from a special kind of superstar…

'That's me!' Jack thought to himself as he sat there on the subs bench, waiting for his chance to shine.

'He is a different type of player to any that we have'. That's what the England manager, Gareth Southgate, had said about Jack after his debut against Denmark in 2020, and it was true. He looked different with his low socks and his slicked-back, curtains hairstyle – and he played the game differently too. Raheem, Marcus Rashford, Jadon Sancho and Bukayo Saka were all attackers with lots of speed and skill, but none of them had Jack's creativity. With the ball at his feet, he was a football wizard! He could glide past defenders like they weren't even there, and spot amazing passes before anyone else could see them.

In the group games, Jack hadn't had the chance to show his magic against Croatia or Scotland, but that changed in England's third game, against the Czech Republic. In the eleventh minute, he collected the ball on the left side of the box, took on two defenders, and then chipped a beautiful cross into the middle for Raheem to head home. *1–0!*

'Jack Grealish delivers!' cried the commentator on the TV.

He had done it once, so could he do it again, a week later in the Round of 16 against Germany? There was only one way to find out. With twenty-five minutes to go, Southgate made his first substitution. Off came Bukayo, and on came England's new

Number Seven… Super Jack!

'Hurraaaaaaaaay!' The fans let out a loud roar as their favourite player entered the field. The belief was back, and the pressure was on.

But it was no problem! Jack had been handling high expectations ever since making his Aston Villa debut at the age of eighteen. The pressure didn't bother him; in fact, it made him raise his game and play even better football.

'Come on, England!'

Jack had only been on the pitch for five minutes when Kyle Walker played the ball forward to Raheem, who dribbled infield and then threaded a pass through to Harry. The England captain had his back to goal and three Germany defenders surrounding him, so…

'Yes, H!' Jack called out, making a run towards the edge of the penalty area, and Harry laid the ball back to him. Now what? Although it was tempting to try and weave his way towards goal like he used to as a kid, instead he went for the safer, wiser option of a simple pass to Luke Shaw, who was sprinting past him up the left wing. Luke fizzed the ball across the six-yard box, and there was Raheem to poke it in. *1–0!*

'Yessssss!' Jack cheered, throwing his arms out wide as he raced over to join the team celebrations. England were winning, and in the Wembley stands above, the supporters were going absolutely wild. What a moment, and what a feeling! Despite representing the Republic of Ireland at youth level, Jack was England born and bred, and he was so proud to be playing for the national football team at last.

Jack wasn't just playing for his country, though; he was starring for it. Only ten minutes later, it was Luke's turn to get the ball in the middle, and Jack's turn to sprint past him up the left wing. 'Yes, Luke!' he called out, and when the pass arrived, Jack curled in a low cross for Harry to score with a diving header. *2–0!*

Jack was lying flat on the grass as the ball landed in the net, but he picked himself back up in a hurry. Because England had a second goal to celebrate, and he had his second assist of the tournament! The fans had called for a special kind of superstar and Jack had delivered.

'Nice one, mate!' Luke shouted, giving him a double high-five, before they both joined the big player pile-on by the corner flag. They were on their way to the Euro 2020 quarter-finals!

'It's coming home, it's coming home, it's coming, FOOTBALL'S COMING HOME!'

At the final whistle, Harry and Raheem hugged each other on the halfway line and then called out to another of England's match-winning heroes:

'Jack, get over here!'

Although he was still a super sub for now, it felt like the start of great things for Jack. At the age of twenty-five, Solihull's favourite son was finally fulfilling his enormous potential – first, for his boyhood club, Aston Villa, and now for his country too.

CHAPTER 2

ALWAYS ASTON VILLA

Solihull, the town where Jack and his family lived, was known for its beautiful old buildings and for being the home of the Land Rover car company. But football? No, the town was definitely not famous for that. The two biggest local clubs, Moor Green and Solihull Borough, both played in the lower Midland leagues, and so young football fans like Jack often supported the more successful teams in the area instead.

West Bromwich was twenty-five miles north-west, home to Championship side West Bromwich Albion...

Coventry was fifteen miles east, home to Premier League team Coventry City...

...And best of all, Birmingham was only ten miles north, home to two big clubs: Aston Villa and Birmingham City.

So, which one would Jack choose to support? St Andrew's, the Birmingham City stadium, was closer to Solihull, but no:

'Aston Villa,' his dad, Kevin, told Jack at a very early age, with no room for doubt. 'Always Aston Villa.'

To make doubly sure, Kevin also gave his son his first claret-and-blue club shirt. But why Aston Villa? Because the link between the football club and Jack's family went a long way back, all the way to 1897.

'That was the year when your great-great grandfather, Billy Garraty, started playing for Villa,' his parents told him. 'Billy was a brilliant goalscoring forward and he stayed at the club for eleven years. In 1903, he even got one cap for England, but his greatest moment came two years later in 1905, when he helped Villa to beat Newcastle United and win the FA Cup.'

Wow – a trophy-winning, international footballer

in his family? Amazing! Jack loved the tale of Billy Garraty, which was a good thing because he would hear it many, many times throughout his childhood. And the story almost always ended in the same way:

'Maybe you'll be the one to follow in his footsteps, Jack!'

And the family connection to the club didn't end there with his great-great grandfather. No – supporting Villa had been passed on from generation to generation, and now Jack's own father was one of the most passionate fans on the planet.

'I was there at Villa Park when we won the league in 1981,' Kevin liked to remind his sons proudly, 'and I was there in Rotterdam when we won the European Cup a year later. What a night that was – unbelievable! And I was there at Wembley when we won the League Cup in 1996 too. We're a happy family of Villa fans – isn't that right, Kevan?'

Jack's older brother Kevan nodded back enthusiastically and then threw his arms up in the air and sang loudly:

'And it's Aston Villa,
Aston Villa FC,
We're by far the greatest team,
The world has ever seen...!'

Kevan was already old enough to go to games with their dad at Villa Park, which was where he'd learned all the famous club chants. Jack was so jealous and desperate to join them.

'Please let me come too!' he begged from the day of his fourth birthday. 'I'm nearly five now!'

Jack was still closer to four than five when his dad finally gave in and took him to his first match. Aston Villa vs Leeds United, in the FA Cup Fifth Round – it was a football game that Jack would never forget.

Just being there in a stadium was an exciting new experience for him. Standing on his seat in the Holte End to get a better view, Jack was surrounded by so many supporters, plus all the fascinating sights and thunderous sounds of live football. Wow, Villa Park was his new favourite place in the world!

'Look, there are the two Gareths: Southgate and

Barry!' Kevan said, pointing out each of the Villa players as they warmed up on the pitch below. 'And there's Benito Carbone – he's Italian and he's incredible!'

Jack listened carefully to his brother and did his best to learn all the names and all the songs. He was already buzzing, and kick-off was still fifteen minutes away.

And it's Aston Villa,
Aston Villa FC,
We're by far the greatest team,
The world has ever seen...!

It turned out to be a brilliant first football match to watch, full of end-to-end entertainment and, most importantly, great goals. At the final whistle, Villa were the 3–2 winners, thanks to a stunning hat-trick from Carbone.

Yes, Kevan had been right about Carbone! For the first goal, he flicked the ball up and volleyed it in from the edge of the box:

Goooooooooooooooooooooaaaaaaaaaaaaaaaaaallllllllllllll lllllllllllll!!!!!!!!!!!!!!!!!!!

For the second, he bamboozled the keeper with a swerving long-range strike:

Goooooooooooooooooooooaaaaaaaaaaaaaaaaaallllllllllllll lllllllllllll!!!!!!!!!!!!!!!!!!!

...And then for the third, the little Italian threw himself forward to score a diving header!

Goooooooooooooooooooooaaaaaaaaaaaaaaaaaallllllllllllll lllllllllllll!!!!!!!!!!!!!!!!!!!

As the ball hit the back of the net, Villa Park went absolutely wild. First, there was an almighty, explosive roar, and then the fans were jumping up and down and hugging each other like they'd just won the FA Cup final.

> *Carbone, oh-oh,*
> *Carbone, oh-oh-oh!*

Jack had never seen or heard anything quite like it.

'So, what did you think, son?' his dad asked as they left the stadium that afternoon.

'It was AMAZING!' Jack replied, his eyes still wide with excitement. 'When can I come again?'

'Well, that depends,' Kevin said with a cheeky smile. 'Do we have another Villa fan in the family?'

'YESSSSSSS!'

Decision made: Jack would always be Aston Villa. He was going to be a fan for life like his dad, and hopefully, a legendary player too one day like his great-great grandfather.

CHAPTER 3

HIGHGATE UNITED'S LITTLE HERO

Soon, Jack had a season ticket of his own, and regularly stood next to his dad and brother at Villa Park. He was a proper, passionate Villa fan now, and he loved every second of it. They would get to the ground extra early so that he could watch the players warm up and stay extra late so that he could wait and meet them after the match. Paul Merson, Dion Dublin, Lee Hendrie, David Ginola – Jack would queue up patiently to get their autographs again and again. And when there wasn't a home match, sometimes the Grealish family even travelled to watch their beloved team play away in other cities across England.

And it's Aston Villa,
Aston Villa FC,
We're by far the greatest team,
The world has ever seen...!

Being a football fan was fun, but for Jack, being a footballer was even better. While he really enjoyed watching his heroes in action every weekend, nothing could beat being on the ball himself. Thanks to hours and hours of practice, plus all that inspiration from his Villa Park idols, he was getting better and better. Every single day, he just wanted to get outside and play:

In the playground at Our Lady of Compassion Roman Catholic Primary School,

In the back garden on his own,

Or in the local park with Kevan and their cousins.

That was Jack's favourite time of the week because it was his chance to test himself against bigger boys. He was the smallest and youngest of all the cousins, but he never let that stop him from showing off his skills. Even at the age of four, he was brilliant at controlling the ball and dribbling with it as if it was glued to his little boot. Weaving his way past opponents was simply the greatest feeling in the whole wide world.

'Tackle him, one of you!' Kevan often cried out in frustration, but it wasn't that easy. On the run, sometimes little Jack was simply unstoppable.

'Nice one, Twinkletoes!' Jack's teammates cheered as he scored another goal.

The older he got, the better Jack became, and the more people stopped to admire him playing in the park.

'Wow, that boy's going to be a superstar!' one man said to his dad. 'Birmingham City should sign him up now!'

But Kevin shook his head firmly. 'No way, my son's going to play for Aston Villa!'

Although he smiled as he said it, he wasn't joking around. No, Kevin was totally serious when it came to his son's special football talent. He saw no reason why Jack couldn't follow in his great-great grandfather's footsteps if he really wanted to.

Before joining the Aston Villa academy, however,

Jack would need a local football club to play for first. Somewhere he could learn more about the game, the tactics and teamwork, while also having lots of fun with friends. One day, Kevin was talking about his talented son to a man who turned out to be a youth coach at a club in Solihull called Highgate United.

'Wow, your boy sounds like a future superstar!' Richard Sweeney replied. 'Why don't you bring Jack down for a trial with our Under-7s at Kings Heath Park?'

'Great, thanks, I will – he'd love that!'

When the morning of the trial arrived, Sweeney was a bit surprised to meet a very small boy wearing an Aston Villa kit that was far too big for him, plus massive shin pads that covered his knees.

'This is my son Jack who I was telling you about.'

Sweeney's first thought was, 'Wow, he's tiny!', but that soon changed to, 'Wow, he's terrific!' once Jack started doing keepie-uppies on the sidelines:

...5... 10... 15... 20...

What a talented five-year-old! Sweeney could already see that the kid really was as good as his dad had said he was. And that was just the start; as the trial went on, Jack grew in confidence, getting better and better until he was dribbling past the older defenders with ease, just like he did with his cousins in the park.

'The boy's a little magician!' the other coaches marvelled.

Jack signed for Highgate United straight away, and he couldn't wait to get started for his first proper football club. Sweeney, however, had some worries about the team's new star. As skilful as he was, was Jack still too small and too young to be playing for the age group above?

It did take Jack a few games to get used to league football, but he didn't struggle for long. Just like at his trial, he grew in confidence, getting better and better, until he was running the show for Highgate United.

'Yes, roll it to me!' Jack called out to his goalkeeper. He wanted to be on the ball as much as possible, even if that meant dropping deep into defence to get it. With the game tied, it was time for a moment of match-winning magic.

With the ball practically glued to his boot, Jack began to dribble his way up the pitch, past one player, then another, then another, as if they were just cones at a training session. Jack was having the time of his life; weaving his way past opponents was simply the greatest feeling in the whole wide world.

'Go on, son!' he could hear his dad urging him on from the touchline. 'All the way!'

He was over the halfway line now, but surely, someone was going to tackle him? No, on the run, little Jack was simply unstoppable. With another flash of fancy footwork, he glided his way past the last defender and into the penalty area, where he smashed a shot past the keeper.

Goooooooooooooooooooooaaaaaaaaaaaaaaaaaallllllllllllllll llllllllllll!!!!!!!!!!!!!!!!!!!!!

CHAPTER 4

SCOUTED
BY VILLA!

'Wow, it's like watching Diego Maradona!' Jim
Thomas thought to himself when he saw Jack's
wondergoal that day.

The kid looked so small in his over-sized orange
shirt, but boy could he play football! He had just
dribbled his way through the entire team, like
Maradona had for Argentina against England at the
1986 World Cup.

But while Thomas was already impressed, it was
too soon to get carried away. 'Let's see if he can do it
again,' the experienced football scout muttered. Over
the years, Thomas had watched so many skilful young
stars create one-off moments of magic, but he wasn't

interested in fluky flashes of brilliance. His job was to find quality footballers who could perform their skills consistently – like winger Lee Sharpe who had gone on to play for Manchester United and Leeds United, and striker Dean Sturridge who had gone on to play for Derby County and Wolves.

So, was Highgate United's little hero good enough to weave his way through and score another wondergoal? Yes, he was! Ten minutes later, he danced his way past every defender again and slotted the ball into the bottom corner. *GOAL!* He made football look so easy and exciting.

'Okay, that boy's definitely one for the future,' Thomas decided. At the end of the game, the scout went straight over to speak to the Highgate United manager, who introduced him to the man of the match's mum.

'Hi there, I'm a football scout and I've been watching your son – he's some player, isn't he?! Would he like to come for a trial at Villa?'

Karen couldn't help laughing at the question. 'You can ask Jack yourself, but I'm pretty sure the answer is yes!'

She was right, of course; Jack's big dream was to become a professional footballer, and there was only one club he really wanted to play for: Aston Villa. Always Aston Villa.

'Mum, this is the best day EVER!' Jack said on the journey home that day. He couldn't wait to tell the rest of his family and all his friends at school – he had been scouted by Villa!

And after impressing the coaches during his trial, he soon started training with the club's Under-7s twice a week. Yes, he was a proper youth team player now, and he had the claret-and-blue kit to prove it.

'I play for Villa!' he told people loudly and proudly.

Jack did miss his old teammates at Highgate United and those matches where he could dribble past every defender with ease, but this was his chance to challenge himself at a higher level, against the best young players in the Birmingham area and beyond.

'This is where I belong,' Jack said to himself before the start of each session, but suddenly he wasn't the stand-out star anymore and he couldn't just win games on his own. When he tried to weave his way through the entire team like he used to, his opponents were talented enough to stop him.

'Come on, kid – lift your head up and look around. If there's no way through, pass the ball!' his coaches kept telling him.

Jack was eager to learn and improve, but at first, he found it hard to adapt to the Aston Villa way. Dribbling was his favourite thing to do and what made football so much fun! It was also what he was best at, and that's why he wanted to be on the ball all the time. So, why did they want him to stop dribbling?

'No, no, we still want you to run with the ball because you're brilliant at it,' the Villa coaches explained, 'but it's about choosing your moments and making the right decisions – when to dribble or shoot yourself, and when it's better to pass or cross the ball to a teammate instead. The best players make the best decisions.'

'Like Juan Pablo Ángel?'

The Colombian striker was Jack's new favourite Villa player, and his sixteen goals had helped the club to finish sixth in the Premier League again.

'Yes, exactly like Ángel!'

'Okay, I'll give it a go.'

Guided by his new hero, Jack worked hard to become a better all-round player. He was starting to see that football was about teamwork and tactics, as well as individual talent. Before long, the Villa coaches were really pleased with his progress.

'That's it – what a ball to Callum. Much better!'

Jack's number one inspiration, though, wasn't Ángel, but Keelan, his younger brother, who had tragically died when Jack was just four years old. It had been a heartbreaking time for the Grealish family, but the memory of his younger brother drove Jack on to achieve his Aston Villa dream – for himself, but also in honour of Keelan.

CHAPTER 5

THE EXCITEMENT
OF EURO 2004

Usually, Jack felt sad when Aston Villa's Premier
League season ended each May, but 2004 was
different. Why? Because soon it would be time for
Euro 2004!

Jack had been too young to really enjoy the 2002
World Cup, but now he was nearly nine years old, the
perfect age to get excited about a major international
tournament. Plus, this time, England had a team that
was really worth getting excited about:

Gary Neville, Sol Campbell, John Terry and Ashley
Cole in defence,

David Beckham, Paul Scholes, Frank Lampard and
Steven Gerrard in midfield,

And up front, Michael Owen and the new wonderkid, Wayne Rooney.

What a star-studded line-up; surely, they were good enough to win the whole tournament! Jack loved all of the England players, but especially Rooney. It was partly because of the way he played the game – the skill, the pace, the power – but also because of his age. Just eighteen – less than ten years older than Jack – and he was already playing for his country!

'That could be me one day,' Jack dared to dream.

Rooney, meanwhile, was living his dream to the max. In England's first match against France, he had the confidence to nutmeg Robert Pirès, 360 spin away from Zinedine Zidane, and flick the ball over Lilian Thuram's head. Unbelievable – the guy was a football genius! And in England's second match against Switzerland, he was even better. Midway through the first half, Owen crossed it in and up jumped Rooney, in between the Swiss centre-backs, to head the ball in. *1–0!*

'Yesssssss!' Jack cheered at home with his family, while out in Coimbra, Portugal, England's new

Number Nine cartwheeled his way over to the corner flag.

Then in the second half, Rooney scored again, and this one was even better. After dribbling his way into the box, he faked to shoot into the far corner, but then caught the keeper out at his near post instead. *2–0!*

Jack sat there staring at the TV screen in awe. Wow, what a strike, and what a superstar! Rooney was only eighteen years old and he'd just scored his second goal for England at Euro 2004, but instead of a wild celebration, he just jogged away smiling.

'Now that is COOL!' Jack and his brother Kevan agreed.

Four days later, they watched together as Rooney put on another man-of-the-match performance in England's final group game against Croatia. He started by setting up a goal for Scholes, and then went on to score two more of his own. The first was a swerving shot from twenty-five yards, but Jack preferred the second. After a one-two with Owen, Rooney ran all the way from the halfway line with the ball and calmly sent the keeper the wrong way.

'That's the kind of goal I like to score for Villa!' Jack thought, and then he tried to imagine himself doing it for England in front of 57,000 supporters at a major international tournament. It seemed impossible, but if Rooney could do it...

The Grealish brothers couldn't wait to see what England's young hero would do next in the quarter-finals against Portugal. Unfortunately, however, Rooney had to hobble off the pitch after only twenty-seven minutes with a foot injury.

'Noooooo,' Jack groaned. 'Now, we're definitely going to lose!'

Sadly, he was right; after extra-time and penalties, Portugal were the winners and England's exciting Euro 2004 adventure was over.

'Never mind, boys – there's always the World Cup in 2006,' Kevin tried to console his sons.

But that was two whole years away! At first, Jack just sat there feeling angry and devastated. If only Rooney hadn't hurt his foot; if only the referee hadn't wrongly disallowed Campbell's header... Football could be so cruel and unfair!

A few days later, however, Jack was feeling better about football again. Maybe it wasn't so bad, after all. Euro 2004 was a tournament that he would remember forever for lots of reasons, but especially because of Wayne Rooney. At the age of eighteen, Rooney had suddenly burst onto the scene as England's new superstar striker and one of the most exciting footballers on the planet.

For a talented young player like Jack, Rooney's exciting rise to the top was just the motivation he needed to keep working hard and dreaming big.

'Come on, Kevan,' he called out to his brother. 'Let's go practise in the garden! You can be the Croatian goalkeeper...'

CHAPTER 6

FOOTBALL OR GAELIC FOOTBALL?

As well as silky football skills, there was one other thing that Jack had in common with his new hero, Wayne Rooney: family from Ireland. Although Jack was born in England, he had grandparents from County Dublin, County Kerry and County Galway, and at the age of ten, that Irish influence led him to take up a brand-new sport: Gaelic football.

'Just give it a go,' his family encouraged him when his football season with the Aston Villa academy had ended. 'We reckon you'll love it.'

And they were right. It took Jack a little while to learn all the rules of the game, but once he did, he soon became a brilliant young player, running the show for John Mitchel's Hurling and Camogie Club in Warwickshire in the same way he did on the football field for Villa Under-12s.

'If you keep going, you could be an All-Ireland champion one day!' said his coach, Michael Healy.

Jack's favourite thing about Gaelic football was the freedom. The pitch was bigger and you could do whatever you wanted with the ball; sometimes, players carried it in their hands like in rugby, sometimes, they bounced it like in basketball; and at other times, they kicked it with their feet like in football. Jack, of course, preferred to play with his feet, and on the run, he was simply unstoppable.

Most of the time, anyway. But Gaelic football could be brutal, especially for a skilful star like Jack. The sport was a lot more physical than football, with shoulder barges, shoves and full body contact all allowed. Opponents often targeted him as John Mitchel's best player, and so when they managed to tackle little Jack, they tackled him hard. Really hard.

WHACK! THUMP! SMACK! CRUNCH!

'Owwwwwwww!'

The first time a player sent him flying to the floor, Jack got up and called for a free kick. But the referee just shook his head and told him, 'This isn't football, son.'

Lesson learned! It was time for Jack to toughen up. After that, no matter how many times he got knocked down in a game, he always got back up and carried on playing. He was having too much fun and scoring too many goals to let a few bumps and bruises stop him.

'Plus, it's all good preparation, son, because when you go back to football, a few kicks will feel like nothing compared to this!' his dad said with a proud smile.

Yes, the more Gaelic football Jack played, the stronger he grew and the better he became at skipping away from tackles at the last second, which was another useful skill to take back to the football pitch. It was now harder than ever for defenders to stop him when he set off on the dribble.

For the next few summers, Jack spent his weekends playing for John Mitchel's in matches all over England, and for his county, Warwickshire, too. In 2009, his team won a major tournament and travelled to Ireland to play during the half-time break in an All-Ireland

quarter-final clash at Croke Park between Dublin
and Kerry. And Jack scored a point, of course, to the
delight of all his Irish family!

Soon after that, however, things started to get more
serious for Jack at the Aston Villa academy. While the
coaches were pleased to see him developing new skills
from a different sport over the summers, they worried
that Gaelic football was too rough and might result in
Jack getting a serious injury. That would be a disaster
for one of their top young talents.

'We think it's time for you to focus on your football,'
they told him. 'If you keep progressing, you've got a great
chance of making it all the way to the first team here.'

Jack had a decision to make: football or Gaelic
football? In the end, the choice was an easy one – for
him, it would always be football, and it would always
be Aston Villa. His dream was to play at Villa Park,
and he was determined to achieve it, even if that
meant saying goodbye to Gaelic football.

'Right, I'm ready to focus on football,' Jack told the
academy coaches at Villa. 'First team, here I come!'

CHAPTER 7

THE NEW
GEORGE BEST

'Have you seen that Grealish lad play yet? Wow, he's unbelievable; we haven't had a kid that good in years!'

By the time Jack turned fourteen, people at Villa were already talking about him as a future first team star, the latest in a long line of home-grown heroes that included Lee Hendrie, Gareth Barry, Darius Vassell and Gabby Agbonlahor. All four had gone on to play for England, but the Aston Villa Academy Director, Bryan Jones, believed that Jack had the potential to become the best of them all.

His touch, his skill, his awareness – it was all exceptional for such a young player, but what made Jack truly special was his magical ability to glide past opponents as if they weren't even there. In fact, he was so gifted with the ball at his feet that his youth coaches often gave up trying to tell him what to do. It was best to just let Jack's natural talent flow, they decided, and if he wanted to get the ball off the goalkeeper and try and go past two, or three, or four opponents in one dazzling dribble, then why not?

'On you go, Jack!'

By then, he was already playing for the age group above, the Under-16s, but as a left winger rather than a central attacking midfielder, to protect him from getting fouled too much. Not that little Jack was frightened of being kicked or bullied; no, thanks to his Gaelic football days, he was totally fearless on the pitch. He just wanted to get the ball and play, and he was happy to take on any defender – the bigger and stronger the better!

'Don't dive in,' coaches warned their players before they faced Jack and his fancy footwork. 'If you do, he'll make you look like a fool!'

The path ahead of Jack was clearly set out – the Under-18s, the Under-19s, then the Reserves, and finally, the Aston Villa First Team, who trained at Bodymoor Heath too. It really wasn't that far away now, especially as the club had a proud history of giving their academy players early experience of Premier League football. Barry had made his senior debut as a seventeen-year-old, Hendrie and Vassell at eighteen, and Agbonlahor at nineteen.

'Well, I'm going to play my first match at sixteen!' Jack told his family, as confident and competitive as ever.

Every time he went to Villa Park with his dad and brother, Jack daydreamed about his debut – standing in the tunnel with his teammates, walking out onto the pitch, absorbing in the atmosphere ahead of kick-off, and of course, anticipating the wondergoal he was going to score, which would send the Holte End supporters wild.

'Soon,' Jack told himself. 'I'll be out there starring soon.'

In the meantime, he had a variety of Villa legends to admire and learn from:

Stiliyan Petrov, with his clever, creative passing...

Ashley Young, with his incredible crosses...

John Carew, with his heading and powerful hold-up play...

And Agbonlahor, with his speed and ability to score important goals (especially in the big Second City Derby against Birmingham)...

'There's just one thing missing,' Jack thought to himself. 'Me, with my deadly dribbling!'

What an amazing all-round attack that would be!

It seemed like a matter of time before Jack joined his heroes on the pitch at Villa Park, but he still had plenty of practice to do first. So, on top of three tough academy training sessions each week and matches at the weekend, Jack also worked hard in his back garden. He had everything he needed at home; his parents had given him a set of cones and a football goal as birthday presents, and his dad had also built him a patio pitch for when the weather was bad. So, Jack was free to play football whenever he wanted, which was almost all of the time.

Why stop when there was always a new trick to master, or a weakness to work on,

Like his left foot:

*If you always use your right, defenders are going
to work you out, son.*

Or his defending:

Come on Jack, you've got to track back too!

Or his decision-making:

Hurry up and SHOOT!

Jack knew that last one was the thing he needed
to work on the most. The problem was that he loved
being on the ball so much that sometimes he spent
too long dribbling, passing and crossing, and wasted
great goalscoring chances. That would have to change,
however, if he wanted to become the new Vassell,
Agbonlahor or Young, or even better, the new George
Best.

Jack was way too young to have seen the legendary
Manchester United and Northern Ireland forward
play, but one night when he was fifteen, he watched
a TV documentary about him. Wow, what a genius!
Jack was blown away. He fell in love with everything
about Best: his great goals, his deadly dribbling skills,
but also his style and attitude. As a small, tricky

winger, defenders often tried to stop him by pushing and kicking him, just like they did to Jack. But Best didn't care and he showed it by wearing his socks down low around his ankles. It was a bold challenge to his bigger, stronger opponents. 'Go on, foul me if you can!' he said, as he weaved his way through and scored yet again.

'Now that is COOL!' Jack told his dad. 'I'm going to wear my socks low like that too!'

Unlike Best, Jack did have to play with shin pads on the pitch, but he managed to find a kid-sized pair that would fit under his rolled-down socks. Perfect, now he was ready to be the new George Best! And it worked. When Jack played particularly well in his next few matches, he decided that the low socks were lucky, and so they stayed and became his style. It was yet another way for Jack to stand out in the Aston Villa academy.

CHAPTER 8

ENGLAND OR IRELAND? PART ONE

Jack was so focused on reaching the Aston Villa first team that he hadn't really thought about international football yet. But suddenly he had a big decision to make because with his rolled-down socks and dazzling displays, he had caught the attention of not just one, but two nations: England and Ireland.

Wow, Jack felt proud to be a young player in demand, but the pressure was on – which country would he choose? Although he had lived in Solihull all his life and given up Gaelic football, the Irish influence still remained strong in his family. Argghhhh – which one... which one? To be honest, Jack didn't really mind, as long he was playing football and he was happy.

'Don't worry, this doesn't have to be your final decision,' his dad reassured him. 'You're allowed to play for one country at youth level and then change your mind later on. If I was you, I would just give them both a go and see which you enjoy more.'

So, that's what Jack did. First, he went for trials with the England Under-15s, but following a freak accident after he collapsed, the doctors sent him home early, without even kicking a ball. Jack was devastated and begged them to let him stay and play, but no, he was told to come back next time instead.

Before the next England camp began, however, Jack had his trial for Ireland, and he loved every minute of it. It helped that one of his Aston Villa academy teammates, Jordan Graham, was there as well, but Jack was a strong, confident character and he got on well with everybody. The other players didn't care about his English accent, especially once they'd seen him play.

Wow, what a talent! Jack blew them away with his vision and skill. In the training sessions, he was simply unstoppable. The full-backs tried to push him onto his weaker left foot, but he just glided past them. And the big centre-backs tried to knock him off the ball, but they soon found out that he was a lot stronger than he looked. For a little guy, his legs were huge!

'Now we know why your socks are so low,' the defenders joked with Jack. 'Because they won't fit over your massive calves!'

The Irish camp was exactly the environment Jack had been hoping for; the players made him feel really welcome and the coaches made him feel really wanted.

'Stick with us, kid – you could be a big player for this country!'

That sounded really exciting, and Jack hadn't heard any more news from England. So, when the Republic of Ireland manager John Morling called him up to the Under-15s squad for the 2010 Tri Nations tournament against Wales and Northern Ireland, Jack said yes straight away. And after impressing as a sub in a 1–0 defeat to Wales, Morling moved him into the starting line-up against Northern Ireland, where he set up three goals in a 5–0 thrashing.

'Thanks, mate,' Jordan yelled as they celebrated together. 'It's great to have you here!'

Jack was an Irish youth international now and he didn't stay in the Under-15s for long. No, his talents were needed in the age groups above. Soon, he was promoted to the Under-16s, and then to the Under-17s, who were attempting to qualify for the 2012 UEFA European Championships. In October 2011, Jack and his teammates travelled to Kazakhstan to take part in the first qualifying round. Even though Jack had only just turned sixteen, a key part of Morling's tactical plan was:

'Get the ball out wide to Jack!'

And it worked. Ireland ran riot in their first game against Liechtenstein, with Jack causing all kinds of trouble.

He curled in a beautiful cross for Sam Byrne to score. *3–0!*

He was fouled as he dribbled into the box and Jonathan Leddy scored from the penalty spot. *4–0!*

He grabbed a goal of his own with a glancing header. *6–0!*

And that was all in the first fifty minutes of the match, before Morling decided to substitute his star man. Nooooo – and Jack didn't want to go off; he was having so much fun!

'Well played, lad,' his manager told him. 'I know you wanted to keep on playing, but we need you fit and firing for Kazakhstan.'

That was now a massive game for Ireland because with a second win, they would make it through to the next round of qualification, even before their tricky final match against the Czech Republic. At half-time, however, Kazakhstan were the team winning 1–0. A draw would probably be enough for Ireland, but a defeat would be disastrous!

In the second half, they attacked and attacked, but the ball just wouldn't go in. Thomas Mulroney hit the crossbar and then Sam and Gary O'Neill both hit the side-netting. And what about Jack? Well, he kept dribbling forwards with the ball and creating chances for his teammates, until eventually, with time running out, he decided to go for goal himself. From twenty yards out, Jack pirouetted his way past his marker and then fired a low shot into the bottom corner. *1–1!*

Goooooooooooooooooooaaaaaaaaaaaaaaaaalllllllllllllll
lllllllllllll!!!!!!!!!!!!!!!!!!!!

With his arms up and a big grin on his face, Jack raced away to celebrate. He had saved the day for Ireland – he was a national hero now!

Next up in the elite qualifying round, however, Ireland faced three tough tests against Serbia, the Netherlands and Albania. They were going to need their little magician more than ever, and as always, Jack was up for the challenge.

'Bring it on!'

Thanks to his dangerous dribbling, Jack earned his team penalties against Serbia and the Netherlands, and he also scored a beauty against Albania. But sadly, despite the best efforts of their brightest spark, Ireland still lost all three matches.

It was all good international experience for Jack, though, and after winning the Irish Under-17 Player of the Year award, he moved onwards and upwards to the Under-18s.

But while Jack was really enjoying life in a green

CHAPTER 9

FROM SUB TO NEXTGEN SUPERSTAR

Meanwhile, back at Aston Villa, everything was going exactly according to plan for Jack. At the age of sixteen, not only was he already getting regular game-time for the Reserves, but the First Team manager was also his new biggest fan!

Whenever Villa had a home game on a Saturday afternoon, Alex McLeish liked to go along and watch the academy matches in the morning. Not only was it nice for the manager to show his support for the club's youth teams, but it was also a good chance for him to check out the most promising players. And one star who stood out straight away was the skilful little kid with the low socks.

'That's Jack Grealish,' one of the academy coaches had told McLeish the very first time he saw him play, and it was a name the Villa manager would never forget.

Wow, what a special talent he was! McLeish stood there mesmerised, waiting for him to get on the ball again. Yes, he had a bit of the George Best about him, but the boy was more like Michael Laudrup, the former Barcelona and Real Madrid midfielder. Because while he clearly loved to dribble, he also had an eye for a killer pass, the kind of defence-splitting ball that no-one else could see or deliver. You couldn't teach that; it was natural footballing talent, and it was beautiful to watch.

'That kid's going to be a superstar,' McLeish and Bryan Jones, the Academy Director, both agreed, 'and we've got to do whatever it takes to keep him here.'

By 2012, however, that was becoming harder and harder to do because big teams like Manchester United were trying their best to sign Jack. Nooooo, Villa couldn't let their best young player leave without a fight! So, what could they do to persuade him to stay and sign a contract? McLeish and Jones knew that Jack and his family loved Aston Villa Football Club very much, so surely a deal could be done.

Eventually, after much discussion, they reached an agreement that worked for everyone. Aston Villa got to keep their top young talent, while Jack got a big new contract and a promotion to the first team squad. Hurray!

Suddenly, he was training alongside his Villa heroes like Stiliyan Petrov and Gabby Agbonlahor, as well as other experienced international stars like Richard Dunne, Emile Heskey, Darren Bent and Robbie Keane. For most young players that would have been a nerve-wracking experience, but not for Jack.

'Bring it on!'

He was just excited to have the chance to prove himself at the highest level. And even when Stiliyan shouted at him for giving the ball away, Jack had the self-belief to bounce straight back and try again. He wasn't going to change the way he played the game; he was just going to become an even better version of himself.

McLeish was very impressed, and with lots of

injuries in midfield, the Aston Villa manager named Jack as a sub for their next home game against Chelsea.

'Mum, Dad – I'm going to be on the bench on Saturday!' Jack proudly told his parents. He had a squad number now – 41 – and he was still only sixteen years old, just like he'd always predicted.

When Saturday arrived, the Grealish family were all there at Villa Park to cheer him on: his mum and dad, his older brother Kevan, and his younger sisters Kiera and Holly. But unfortunately, they didn't get to see Jack make his senior debut. With Chelsea leading 2–0, McLeish decided to go for the experience of Heskey rather than the magic of young Grealish. Oh well, it was still good to get a taste of what was to come.

'It's only a matter of time, son,' his dad assured him. 'Just keep going!'

At the end of the 2011–12 season, however, McLeish left Villa and sadly the new manager, Paul Lambert, had a very different plan. With the club fighting relegation, there was no room in the first team for a young flair player like Jack.

'I can't believe it – I didn't even get a squad number

this year!' he complained angrily to his family.

Getting frustrated wasn't going to achieve anything, though. If Jack really wanted to prove Lambert wrong, he would just have to perform well in the Premier League 2 and at the NextGen Series, an exciting new tournament featuring the best Under-19 teams from all over Europe, including:

Barcelona from Spain,

Inter Milan and Juventus from Italy,

Ajax and PSV from the Netherlands,

Borussia Dortmund from Germany,

Sporting Lisbon from Portugal,

And from England: Liverpool, Tottenham, Manchester City, Arsenal, Chelsea and... Aston Villa!

Jack couldn't wait to get started. Most of his teammates were two years older than him, but he was used to being one of the youngest by now, along with his best mate Callum Robinson. Besides, age was just a number; what mattered was footballing talent, and everyone knew Jack had lots and lots of that.

'This could be a big, break-out tournament for you,' the coach Tony McAndrew told him, handing him the

Number 11 shirt.

Despite losing their first two matches, Aston Villa bounced back to win three of their last four games and finish second in their group. And although Jack didn't score a single goal himself, he was at the heart of a lot of Villa's best attacking play, especially in their 5–1 thrashing of Sporting Lisbon. Early in the second half, Jack dribbled all the way through the Portuguese defence with the ball almost glued to his boot, before setting up his fellow Irish international Mikey Drennan for an easy tap-in.

'Thanks, mate – that was magic!' he cheered, giving Jack a big hug.

And on the mighty young Villains marched; past Ajax, one of the most famous football academies in the world, then past the Greek giants Olympiakos, and into the NextGen Series semi-finals, where they faced Sporting Lisbon again. Could Villa cruise to another thrashing? No, on this occasion, the two teams were much more closely matched. The score was 0–0 after forty-five minutes and then 1–1 after ninety. The game was going to extra-time...

'Keep going, lads!' McAndrew told the tired Villa players in the team huddle, before turning to his young attackers. 'Jack, Callum – we could do with some magic from you now!'

Coming up! Seconds after the restart, Callum got the ball on the left and dribbled past two opponents, towards the Sporting penalty area. As he reached the edge of the box, he looked up to see who was in the middle for a cross – two tall defenders versus one little Jack. But Callum knew how clever his best mate was, and so with a swoosh of his right foot, he curled the cross in anyway.

As the ball flew through the air, Jack made his move, escaping behind the Sporting defenders and into space at the back post. Callum's cross was excellent, and so was Jack's first touch to bring the ball down beautifully.

'Now SHOOT!' McAndrew and the other Villa players were thinking, but Jack showed the calm and confidence to wait for the keeper to dive first, before firing the ball into the empty net. *2–1!*

Goooooooooooooooooooooaaaaaaaaaaaaaaaaallllllllllllllll llllllllll!!!!!!!!!!!!!!!!!!

'Yessssssss!' Jack cried out as he raced over to the sideline like a superstar. As he ran, he pointed two fingers to the sky as a tribute to Keelan and then blew kisses to his family in the crowd. It was his heroic moment, and he was determined to enjoy it. Their manager had asked for magic and Callum and Jack had delivered!

Were Villa now on their way to the NextGen final? To make totally sure, Jack set up his captain, Samir Carruthers, to score a third goal. Game over – Villa were victorious! At the end, there were hugs and high-fives, but no wild celebrations yet. 'One more win and that trophy is ours, boys!' Samir clapped and cheered as they left the pitch.

Villa went into the final as underdogs against a strong Chelsea side featuring Andreas Christensen, Nathan Aké, Ruben Loftus-Cheek and Lewis Baker, but they soon showed they had plenty of quality players too, to go with a winning team spirit.

Callum won the first penalty in the forty-ninth minute, after a clumsy tackle from Alex Davey, and up stepped Graham Burke to score from the spot. *1–0!*

Then Jack won the second penalty in the ninety-second minute. After terrorising the Chelsea defence all game long, he decided to go for one last dribble from near the halfway line, and the only way they could stop him was to foul him in the box. Graham grabbed the ball and beat the keeper again. *2–0!*

Now, the wild celebrations could start – because against the odds, Aston Villa had gone all the way to become the 2013 NextGen Winners! It was an amazing achievement that the players would remember proudly for the rest of their lives. Every single one of them had played their part, but there was one young star who had stood out yet again: Jack.

CHAPTER 10

LEARNING ON LOAN

After his NextGen success, Jack went into the 2013–14 season with high hopes. Surely, now he was all set to make his debut for the Villa first team? But no, in mid-September, Lambert decided that he still wasn't ready, and so he sent Jack out on loan to Notts County instead.

Notts County's manager, Chris Kiwomya, had been there at the NextGen final watching his nephew, Alex, play for Chelsea, but the kid who had impressed him most was Aston Villa's Number 11. He moved the ball around with so much class and creativity, but how would he cope against bigger, stronger defenders? There was only one way to find out, and League

One would be the perfect place for him to learn and improve.

'Sure!' Jack agreed straight away. He didn't want to leave Villa, even on loan, but now that he was eighteen, he was desperate to start playing first-team football as soon as possible. This would be an exciting new challenge for him, plus Notts County wasn't too far from his family home in Solihull.

'I can even drive you there and back,' his dad said, as supportive as ever.

So, as Jack arrived at his first Notts County training session, he was feeling positive about the season ahead. First things first, he knew he needed to prove that he wasn't just an arrogant, young Premier League prince who thought he was way better than everyone else.

That's exactly what the more experienced Notts County players were thinking when Jack showed up with his cheeky smile, slicked-back hair and rolled-down socks. But luckily, that first impression didn't last long, because he was confident enough to chat with everyone, and he had the skills to back up his style.

'Woah, this lad is the real deal!' the captain Alan
Sheehan realised as soon as he saw Jack dribble
with the ball, and so did the other new kid in the
Notts County squad. Callum McGregor was a young
midfielder from Celtic who was also on loan for the
season, and they struck up a friendship straight away,
both on and off the football pitch. Jack and Callum,
Notts County's new Number 7 and 8 – and the
supporters were excited to see them in action together.

It was so far so good for Jack at his new club, but
he soon discovered that League One could be a very
difficult division for small players who liked to dribble.
Seconds after making his debut as a second-half
sub against MK Dons, he was flying through the air
following a very strong tackle.

'Argghhhhh – that's got to be a foul!' Jack
complained at first, but when the referee waved play
on, he got back up and carried on. It was all part of his
learning curve. League One was like Gaelic football all
over again; he was just going to have to be brave and
get used to being kicked around.

And another thing that Jack would have to get used

to was losing. In his first eight games at Notts County, the team only won twice as they dropped all the way to the bottom of the league. Although Jack had managed to set up a couple of goals, he was struggling to be the consistent playmaker that the fans were crying out for.

'Stop messing around with the ball and pass it!'

'Come on, kid – you've got to move it quicker than that. This isn't kids' football anymore!'

'Stop being lazy and get stuck in!'

Arggghhh, Jack's loan spell at Meadow Lane was turning into a nightmare!

Things had to change and so in late October, the club sacked Kiwomya and replaced him with Shaun Derry. The new Notts County manager needed to get his team winning again, but how? He could easily have just stuck with the more experienced stars, but after watching Jack in his first training session, Derry decided to take a different approach. He saw a very special young player who would make some mistakes, but who could also produce moments of absolute magic.

'We've got to believe in him,' his assistant manager, Greg Abbott, agreed.

So, Jack stayed on the pitch for the full ninety minutes against Bradford and Brentford, even when he was playing poorly and the team was losing. Despite the frustration of the fans, his manager stuck by him, trusting him to shine.

And he did. A week later, Notts County were desperately clinging on to a 2–1 lead against Gillingham, thanks to two goals from Callum, when the ball flew towards Jack just outside the box. His teammates were calling for him to cross it back in, but instead, he chested the ball down and began to dribble,

Past one player,

Then another,

And then another,

Before firing a shot past the keeper. *3–1!*

Gooooooooooooooooooooooaaaaaaaaaaaaaaaalllllllllllllll llllllllllll!!!!!!!!!!!!!!!!!!!

His first goal at last, and what a way to score it! With joy and relief buzzing through his body, Jack pointed to the sky for Keelan and then raced over to celebrate with two other very important people:

First, his dad, who was there to cheer him on as always,

And then, Derry, his manager, who had believed in him.

'Cheers, Boss!' he said as they hugged on the touchline.

That wondergoal against Gillingham was a turning point for Jack, and for the whole team too. Thanks to his goals, assists, and all-round creativity, Notts County beat Colchester, Bradford, Sheffield United and Stevenage. They were still bottom of League One, but now by only one point. The great escape was on!

Jack's loan spell was supposed to end in January, and he had other offers from Championship clubs, but he turned them all down to remain at Notts County for the rest of the season. He had a job to finish.

'Come on, we can still stay up!' he urged his teammates on.

In March, that looked like mission impossible, but with six wins out of their last eight, Notts County slowly made their way up the table and out of the relegation zone. It was a miracle! On the final day, they just needed to avoid defeat away at Oldham Athletic, and they would be safe in League One for another season.

In the first half, however, Jack played like it was any other game, taking too many risks and only jogging back to defend. Why wasn't he taking things more seriously? Was this match too important for a young loan player like him? Was it time to take him off? No, instead, Abbott spoke to him at half-time.

'Listen, today's match is massive for us. I know you just want to get on the ball and dribble, but you need to understand what this means to the club. If we lose, we go down, and that will have a disastrous effect on everyone at the club. You've really helped us to get this far, but now we need one last push. The only way we'll stay up is if everyone works together. Okay?'

Jack nodded and in the second half, he came out fighting for his team. When Oldham took the lead, he pushed Notts County forward on the attack again. Finding two defenders in front of him, Jack passed the ball wide to Jamal Campbell-Ryce instead, whose cross

struck a defender on the arm. *Handball! Penalty!* Up
stepped Alan to score the equaliser. *1–1!*

'Get in!' Jack screamed as the Notts County players
celebrated in front of their fans, and together, they
held on until the final whistle blew. They had done it;
they were staying up!

Five goals, seven assists, and hundreds of highs,
lows and lessons learned – it was a first season of
professional football that Jack would never forget.

CHAPTER 11

FIRST SEASON IN THE VILLA FIRST TEAM

Jack had left Aston Villa as a boy and he was returning as a man. Not only was he now taller and stronger, but he was also more mature and focused after a year of first-team football at Notts County. All the coaches could see the difference straight away, including Paul Lambert. And so just four days after his final game in League One against Oldham Athletic, Jack found himself on the bench in the Premier League against Manchester City. It was a good thing that nothing fazed him!

'It's great to be back,' Jack said to his best mate Callum Robinson, who was a substitute too. 'Maybe I'll finally get to make my Villa debut today!'

The two teams were level at half-time, but when City went 2–0 up in the second half, Jack's wish grew more and more likely. Surely it was time for Villa to give their top youngsters a chance?

In the seventy-ninth minute, off came Ciaran Clark and on came Callum.

And in the eighty-eighth minute, off came Ryan Bertrand and on came… Jack!

At last, the moment he had been waiting years for! But unfortunately, there was to be no super sub dream debut. Instead, within seconds of Jack entering the pitch, City scored a third goal through Stevan Jovetić and then a fourth through Yaya Touré.

'Welcome to the Premier League!' Jack thought to himself as his shoulders slumped.

Oh well, at least he was finally up and running as an Aston Villa first-team player. This was just the beginning for him; hopefully, 2014–15 would be the season he became a superstar.

However, despite impressing in preseason training, Jack found himself on the bench again once the Premier League resumed. For all his flashes of magic, the manager preferred to pick Andreas Weimann and Charles N'Zogbia as his first-choice wingers for now.

'Get Grealish on!' the Villa fans still yelled during each and every match. They were desperate to see more of their home-grown hero and his entertaining style of play.

Lambert refused to rush things, though. He gave Jack twenty minutes against Stoke City, then fifteen against Hull City, then forty-five against Arsenal, then twenty minutes against Manchester City... He was glad to get more Premier League experience, but how was Jack supposed to show what he could really do when he never got a proper chance to play?

'Get Grealish on from the start!' the fans now began to shout, as Villa dropped lower and lower down the league table.

Just like at Notts County, a new manager would make all the difference for Jack. In February 2015, Lambert left the club and Tim Sherwood took over. In his previous job at Tottenham, Sherwood had given Harry Kane his first Premier League start, so would he do the same with Villa's own local lad?

'I can see you're capable of special things,' Jack's new manager told him at training, 'but now it's time to show it in matches. When you get the ball, be brave and do what you do best: take defenders on and beat them.'

'Yes, boss!'

Jack got his first chance to impress Sherwood in the FA Cup Sixth Round against Midland rivals, West Brom. Villa were already 1–0 up when he came on, but he helped secure the victory by dribbling forward from his own half and setting up Scott Sinclair to score.

'Yesssssss!' Jack screamed up at the sea of Villa supporters as he jumped on Scott's back. What a feeling!

Even a harsh second yellow card for diving, and the red card that followed, couldn't spoil Jack's night. Not only were Villa on their way to Wembley for the semi-finals, but his super sub performance had put even more pressure on Sherwood to give him his first Premier League start.

Jack stayed on the bench for the defeats against Swansea City and Manchester United, but suddenly

QPR at home had become a must-win match for Villa.

'Congratulations, you're starting tonight,' Sherwood told Jack, expecting him to be excited and thankful.

But no, his cheeky reply was: 'About time!'

Although Christian Benteke was Villa's hat-trick hero against QPR, Jack played well enough to keep his starting spot for the rest of the Premier League season, and for the FA Cup semi-final too. Wow, Liverpool at Wembley – it was a huge game with so much hype and expectation. With the pressure on, would Jack dazzle or disappoint?

Dazzle, of course! He seemed to save his best performances for the biggest games. So what if it was Wembley? Jack was just having fun playing football. Every time he got the ball, he attacked with speed and skill, and the excitement grew amongst the Villa supporters. What a talent! What would he do next? He was causing Liverpool lots of problems, and he even had the confidence to drop deep and pick the ball up off his own defenders, like he used to do for the Villa youth team.

Then came the match-winning magic. Moments

after Liverpool had taken the lead, Jack dribbled up the left wing and threaded a perfectly weighted ball through to Fabian Delph, who crossed it in to Christian. *1–1!*

What a great goal! Fabian and Christian were the first to embrace, but then they turned to wait for their third member.

'Nice one, Jacky!'

And Villa's dream team weren't done yet. Early in the second half, Christian flicked the ball back to Jack on the edge of the Liverpool box. On his Wembley debut, in front of 85,000 fans, Jack somehow showed the composure and vision to spot Fabian on the run and find him with an inch-perfect pass. Fabian then cut inside brilliantly and slammed a shot into the bottom corner. *2–1!*

Comeback complete – Villa were winning and Jack was having the game of his life! After eighty-four magical minutes, his day was done and he walked off the pitch to a standing ovation from the crowd. Already, he was a fan favourite!

'Listen to the roar and look at his name,' exclaimed

the commentator on TV, 'because you're going to hear a lot more about this young man.'

Ten anxious minutes later, Jack was back on the field, celebrating a famous victory. Villa were in the FA Cup Final!

And when the big day arrived, Sherwood stuck with the same attack again: Fabian, Charles, Christian… and Jack! He was starting and his whole family were there at Wembley to cheer him on in his biggest game yet. Was he about to follow in the footsteps of his great-great-grandfather, Billy Garraty?

'Good luck, son!' Kevin told him. 'I've seen Villa win the league, the European Cup and the League Cup, but never the FA Cup. Today's the day that changes!'

Sadly, however, it turned out to be a disappointing day for Jack, his dad and all Villa players and fans. Arsenal dominated the final from minute one, with Villa defending desperately. They managed to hold on until the fortieth minute, but after that, the Arsenal goals flooded in:

Theo Walcott volleyed home. *1–0!*

Alexis Sánchez scored a screamer. *2–0!*

Per Mertesacker headed in. *3–0!*

Game over. Jack stayed on for the full ninety minutes, but as hard as he tried, there was nothing he could do to turn things around for his team. And to make matters even worse, Arsenal added a fourth goal (from Olivier Giroud) just before the final whistle.

'Noooooo!' Jack sank to the floor and sat with his head bowed, staring at the grass below his boots. There was only one word for how he felt in that moment: gutted. He had gone into the game with such high hopes, but instead, Villa had been humiliated in the FA Cup Final. All Jack could do was collect his runners-up medal and learn from the experience. His first season in the Villa first team had been a real rollercoaster ride, but hopefully, his second would be all highs and no lows.

CHAPTER 12

ENGLAND OR IRELAND?
PART TWO

Before the 2015–16 season had started, however, Jack
once again became the subject of an international tug
of war. Now that he was becoming a Premier League
star, the pressure was mounting for him to make the
big, final decision about which senior team to play for.
Which country would he choose: England or Ireland?

So far, Jack had stayed loyal to Ireland, from the
Under-15s all the way through to the Under-21s. He
had always enjoyed wearing the green shirt because of
his family background, and the FAI had always treated
him very well, making him feel important and offering
him the chance to play for older age groups. In Jack's
head it was simple; why would he want to join the

England Under-19s when he could play for the Ireland Under-21s instead?

'I made up my mind a few months ago that Ireland was the best for me,' Jack told the media in 2013, 'and I'm happy with the decision.'

A year later, however, when the national team manager Martin O'Neill invited him to train with the senior squad ahead of a friendly against Oman, Jack decided to stay with the Under-21s instead. Why? Had he changed his mind? Didn't he want to become an Ireland international anymore?

'It's a big decision to make and one I want to take my time over,' Jack explained, but that didn't stop the rumours from spreading:

Is Grealish about to switch and play for England instead?

Until then, international football had been all about having fun for Jack, but suddenly, things were getting serious. At the time, Roy Keane was his assistant manager for both club and country, and so Keane was constantly telling him, 'Keep playing for Ireland!'

Jack refused to rush, though. His next step would

be really important because that decision would mean forever. England or Ireland – once he made his senior debut for one country, there was no going back to the other. Jack had to be sure he was doing the right thing, and so he decided to keep his options open and take a year away from international football to think.

As soon as Jack broke into the Aston Villa first team in early 2015, however, the two national teams began fighting over him again. In March, Ireland named Jack as their Under-21 Player of the Year, and two months later, after his FA Cup masterclass against Liverpool, O'Neill offered him another senior call-up.

'We appreciated the call from Martin yesterday but there was no way Jack was going to accept,' his dad replied for him.

England, meanwhile, sent several of their top youth coaches to speak to Jack and his family, including Gareth Southgate, the Under-21 manager, and Kenny Swain, an Aston Villa legend.

'We just want you to know that you're on our radar and we rate you very highly,' they told him, trying not to put too much pressure on him.

England or Ireland? Arghhhhh, Jack didn't know which country to choose! It was definitely the most difficult decision of his football career so far. His dad, however, seemed to be enjoying the situation. 'There's a friendly coming up,' Kevin joked with the journalists. 'You never know, he could play forty-five minutes for Ireland and forty-five minutes for England, half and half."

But in fact, when the two nations faced each other on 7 June 2015, Jack played for… neither team! Ireland had hoped that he'd make his debut, but no, it was too soon. He still needed more time to think before making his big final decision.

Significantly, it was Roy Hodgson, the England senior team manager, who made the next move later that summer. On 14 August, he travelled to Villa Park to watch Aston Villa vs Manchester United, but also to have a secret meeting with Jack, who was injured for the match.

'Look, kid, I'm not here to guarantee you a place in the England team,' Hodgson said honestly. 'I would never say that to any player because it would be a lie. But the truth is that we've been watching your progress for a long time and we'd love for you to be a part of England's future.'

Jack was delighted to hear those words from Hodgson, but at the same time, he couldn't walk away from Ireland without having a similar meeting with O'Neill. That wouldn't be fair after everything they'd done for him during his younger years, and all the patience they'd shown.

'We all know that you're a talented lad,' the Ireland manager told him, 'but realistically, you're going to play more games for us than you are for England. We've got a great chance of qualifying for Euro 2016 and you could be a key player in getting us there.'

Interesting! Now that he'd heard both sides of the argument, it was time for Jack to make his decision at last. But before he did, he went to ask his Villa manager for some advice.

'At the end of the day, you've got to do whatever feels right for you,' Tim Sherwood told him. 'If you love playing for Ireland and that's where you want to stay, then do that. But believe me, you are good enough to play for England if you choose to. And I know they haven't been brilliant in recent years, but they qualify for every major tournament and they're still one of the best national teams in the world.'

'Thanks, Boss – I think I've made up my mind.'

On 28 September, Jack finally announced his international switch: 'It was not an easy decision as Ireland has a special place with me through my family. However, I have decided to represent the country of my birth.'

Yes, Jack had lived in Solihull his whole life, and ever since watching Wayne Rooney at Euro 2004, his dream had always been to play for England. That was his target now, no matter how long it might take.

CHAPTER 13

GUTTED TO GO DOWN

Now that Jack had chosen England, his next task was to earn his first call-up to the Under-21 squad. It wasn't going to be easy to break into a squad filled with amazing young attackers like Harry Kane, Jesse Lingard and Ruben Loftus-Cheek, but if he played well in the Premier League, hopefully he could do it.

Before that, however, Jack needed to get his mind fully focused on football – no more bad behaviour off the pitch, and no more negative newspaper headlines.

'You're one of the best young players I've ever worked with, and I'd hate to see you waste your talent,' Tim Sherwood told him sternly. 'It's time to start acting like a proper professional; you're nearly twenty years old now.'

The 2015–16 season was all set to be a crucial one for Jack, and for Aston Villa too. The previous year, they had avoided relegation by just three points, and now they had lost two of their key players: Fabian to Manchester City and Christian to Liverpool. The club had signed new players to replace them, but in order to stay up again, they were relying on their home-grown hero to really shine.

'Grealish is going to save us!' the Villa supporters hoped.

It was a lot of pressure to put on a young player, and Jack could only show flashes of his brilliance. Away at Leicester City, there was chaos in the box, with the ball pinging around everywhere. When it finally came out to Jack on the edge, however, he calmly curled a first-time shot through the crowded penalty area and into the corner of the net. *1–0!*

Goooooooooooooooooooaaaaaaaaaaaaaaaaallllllllllllllll llllllllllll!!!!!!!!!!!!!!!!!!!!

What a touch of class, what a moment of magic! It was Jack's first-ever senior goal in a Villa shirt, and so with his fists pumping, he raced over to the touchline and jumped into his manager's arms.

'Yes, kid!' Sherwood shouted in Jack's ear. 'I knew you could do it!'

And he wasn't the only one who believed in Villa's boy wonder; so did the supporters, who chanted his name loud and proud:

> *Super, Super Jack,*
> *Super, Super Jack,*
> *Super, Super Jack,*
> *Super Jacky Grealish!*

But unfortunately, one great goal wasn't going to be enough to save Villa. They had problems all over the pitch; their new strikers weren't scoring, their defenders were making too many mistakes, and the whole team was playing without spirit or confidence. From 2–0 up, they ended up losing 3–2 to Leicester,

Then losing 1–0 to West Brom,

Then losing 3–2 to Liverpool,

Then losing 1–0 to Stoke City…

'Booooooooooooooooooooooooooooo!' the Villa fans jeered. With ten games played, their team sat bottom of the Premier League table with only four points – one win, one draw, and eight defeats. And Jack's own record was even worse: seven games played, seven games lost. It was supposed to be his season to shine, but instead, he was struggling to make an impact or win a single match, and his team was falling apart.

'At this rate, we'll be relegated by Christmas!' Jack groaned with fear and frustration.

Villa needed to turn things around fast, and so in late October, they sacked Sherwood and replaced him with Frenchman Rémi Garde. The new manager wanted his players to be very disciplined and defensively solid, and so unfortunately, he wasn't a fan of Jack's fun-loving football style.

'He just told me off for smiling!' he complained to Gabby.

Sadly, however, Garde couldn't find a way to fix the problems and get Villa winning again. If anything, their results were getting worse, and Jack could only see his beloved club going in one direction – down.

It was a horrible feeling, and after losing his ninth game in a row, Jack was so fed up that he let his football focus slip again. While the rest of the Villa squad returned to Birmingham, he went out partying in Manchester instead.

When Garde found out about Jack, he was furious. It was the last thing that Villa needed with the team in so much turmoil. Jack was in big trouble again! The manager dropped him from the first team for two matches and made him train with the Under-21s.

'You have to behave as a professional and it was not the case this time for Jack,' Garde told the media, using very similar words to ones Sherwood had used. 'He has got a lot of ability but he needs to improve his game and work at it.'

Had Jack learned his lesson at last? Hopefully, but due to injuries and illnesses, he only made another seven appearances that season, and his team lost every single one of them. It was a new Premier League record – sixteen games, sixteen defeats – and not the kind that Jack was hoping for.

Villa, meanwhile, finished bottom of the league

with just seventeen points, the fourth lowest total ever. For the first time in twenty-eight years, the club was dropping down to the Championship and there was nothing Jack could do to save them. 'Relegated' – that word was a crushing blow, especially for a lifelong Villa fan like him. He had tried his best to be their home-grown hero, but he had failed and he felt like he'd let everyone down.

What a miserable year! As Jack walked off the pitch after the final game of the season, he covered his face with his shirt to hide the pain. But even at that lowest moment, he had the strength and belief to make a promise to himself and to all the Villa supporters:

'We'll be back.'

CHAPTER 14

TOULON TOURNAMENT 2016

At the end of that long, dark and difficult season, though, there was at least some good news for Jack. Despite all those defeats with Villa, he had achieved his other aim: a call-up to the England Under-21s!

That summer, they were competing in the Toulon Tournament, a famous international youth competition held in France each year. Alan Shearer, Thierry Henry and Cristiano Ronaldo were just three of the many future superstars who had won the tournament in the past.

Could Jack be next? The England manager, Gareth Southgate, could only select twenty players, but with Lingard and Kane now in the senior team, there was space for another skilful attacker in the squad.

'Look, I'm in!' Jack told his parents proudly, showing them his name on the list. 'I'm going to France!'

While he was the only player from Aston Villa, Jack already knew a lot of his new teammates from the Premier League and from his academy days too. Lewis Baker and Ruben Loftus-Cheek had both been in the Chelsea team they'd beaten in the 2013 NextGen final, while Nathan Redmond had starred for Villa's local rivals, Birmingham City.

'Hey, we're all friends and teammates now!' they joked together.

Jack was really enjoying his first experience with England, but as the training camp stage ended, he looked ahead to the tournament itself. As the new kid in the squad, how much game-time would he get?

In England's first game against Portugal, it was Ruben who started in the Number 10 role, but for their second game against Guinea, Southgate gave Jack his full debut, playing in behind Nathan and Fulham striker Cauley Woodrow.

'Let's do this!' they cheered as they prepared for kick-off.

Guinea took a surprise lead after just fifty seconds, but after that, it was all about England's exciting attackers. They moved the ball forward with speed and skill and they finished with style, again and again.

Nathan played the ball through to Cauley, who crossed it towards Jack at the back post. The defender won the header, but Jack volleyed home the rebound. *1–1!*

Goooooooooooooooooooooaaaaaaaaaaaaaaaaalllllllllllllll llllllllllll!!!!!!!!!!!!!!!!!!!!

Jack was already off the mark in an England shirt! There were no wide smiles or wild celebrations, though; he just jogged back to the halfway line with a focused look on his face, high-fiving teammates along the way. They were just getting started:

Cauley set up Nathan, who fired a long-range rocket past the keeper. *3–1!*

Cauley's cross travelled all the way through to Jack, who cut inside and found the bottom corner. *4–1!*

Goooooooooooooooooooooaaaaaaaaaaaaaaaaalllllllllllllll llllllllllll!!!!!!!!!!!!!!!!!!!!

With a little smile, he pointed over at Cauley and

then gave him a quick hug to say thanks.

Jack was on a hat-trick now, but he wasn't that interested in the individual glory. When Nathan passed him the ball just inside the box, he faked to shoot and played it across to Cauley instead, whose shot deflected in off a defender. *5–1!*

Jack dribbled through the middle at speed and then once again fed the ball to Cauley. *6–1!*

'Cheers, mate,' the striker thanked him with a hug. 'We make a pretty good team, don't we!'

After sixty minutes, Jack's England debut was done, but he was delighted with his two goals and two assists. Not bad for the new kid!

For the next match against Paraguay, however, Ruben was back in the Number 10 role, and he grabbed two goals and an assist. The battle was really on between Ruben and Jack to be England's main playmaker! Jack played in the final group game against Japan, but had he done enough to impress his manager?

Four wins out of four meant England were through to the Toulon Tournament Final, where they faced the hosts, France. So, which of his midfield magicians would Southgate choose for the biggest match of all? In the end, he went for Ruben's experience, and it turned out to be a wise decision because he scored their winning goal. Final score: 2–1. England were the winners!

Although Jack was disappointed not to play at all in the final, he was still very proud to be part of such a talented and successful team. After all, they were the first England team to win the Toulon Tournament in twenty-two years!

When the final whistle blew, Jack raced onto the pitch with the other subs to join in the big squad celebrations, which went on and on all night.

Campeones, Campeones, Olé! Olé! Olé!
England! England! England!

'Great win in the final. Brilliant team performance. Nice to end the season on a high,' Jack posted on social media, along with a photo of him and Nathan, two Birmingham boys living their international football dream together.

Jack now hoped the Toulon Tournament would be the first of many exciting England experiences – and the first of many trophies.

CHAPTER 15

CHALLENGING TIMES IN THE CHAMPIONSHIP

After his impressive performances at the Toulon
Tournament, Jack had several Premier League clubs
chasing him. Surely he was too good to go down
with the rest of the Aston Villa team? Stoke City in
particular were looking to add more creativity to their
midfield, while Everton and Tottenham were also
keeping a close eye on him.

So, as the new 2016–17 season started, Jack had
another difficult decision to make – stay loyal to
his boyhood club and lead them back up to the top
division, or stay in the Premier League with another
team? The new Villa manager, Roberto Di Matteo,
refused to comment on the transfer rumours, but he

did say, 'I think he is a talented boy and I think he has a future here.'

That was exactly what Jack wanted to hear, and he was soon enjoying himself in the Championship. During their first home game of the season, he dribbled into the box, past two Rotherham defenders, and then past the keeper too, before passing the ball into the empty net.

Goooooooooooooooooooooaaaaaaaaaaaaaaaaalllllllllllllll llllllllllll!!!!!!!!!!!!!!!!!!!!!

In moments like that, Jack made football look so effortless and magical. 'Come onnnnn!' he cried out as he jumped over the advertising boards and hugged the happy Villa fans.

> *Super, Super Jack,*
> *Super, Super Jack,*
> *Super, Super Jack,*
> *Super Jacky Grealish!*

His mind was made up. 'Everyone knows this is a club I love dearly, and it's a place I want to play my football,' Jack said as he signed a new four-year contract with Villa. 'We're looking to return to the Premier League. I want to be a big part of that process and will be doing everything possible to make that a reality.'

Initially, Villa's chances of promotion weren't looking good – only one win in their first eleven games. In fact, they were a lot closer to going down than going up! The club was in crisis, so Di Matteo left and in came Steve Bruce, a manager with a lot more experience. Could he lead them back to the Premier League where they belonged?

When Jack was at his best, Villa were capable of anything. Against Wolves, he played a lovely one-two with Ross McCormack and then burst into the box, where a defender dragged him down. *Penalty! 1–0!*

'Great work, Jack!' Bruce shouted from the sidelines.

But could his manager rely on him to be a key and consistent player for the team? No, not yet. Later in the same game, Jack went from hero to villain. After being fouled again, he lost his cool and kicked out at the Wolves defender, Conor Coady. Although the referee on the pitch didn't spot it, the TV cameras did, and afterwards, he received a three-game ban.

'Nooooo, that means I'll miss the Birmingham match!' Jack groaned when he checked the fixture list. What a disaster! It was his dream to score the winner for Villa in the Second City Derby, but now, because of one silly mistake, he would have to wait until the rematch in six months' time.

For Jack, life in the Championship wasn't turning out to be as easy as he'd expected. He still had a lot to learn, especially about staying calm and staying consistent. One week against Wigan Athletic, he cut inside and curled a stunning shot into the top corner to win the game for Villa, but in the next match against Norwich City, he was nowhere near as good and his team lost 1–0.

'Come on, Jacky, we need more of your magic!' the supporters yelled out in frustration because they knew how good their home-grown hero could be. Why wasn't he able to produce those top performances every week?

Nottingham Forest away summed up Jack's up-

and-down season. Midway through the first half, he set up the opening goal for Jonathan Kodjia, but sixty minutes later, he was sent off for a second yellow card, and Villa went on to lose 2–1 without him.

'Not again!' the supporters moaned as their team dropped down to fourteenth place.

Jack, meanwhile, dropped down to the bench for the next two months. Steve Bruce picked the more reliable Henri Lansbury in the playmaker role instead, and suddenly Villa went on a winning run. Were they better off without Jack?

At the age of twenty-one, Jack had reached a real make or break moment in his football career. How many more chances would he get at Villa, how many more mistakes would he be allowed to make? If Jack didn't watch out, he was in danger of wasting his tremendous talent, just like Tim Sherwood had said.

Fortunately, Bruce brought Jack back in for the last six games and he finished the season in good form with super strikes against Fulham and Brighton. And at last, he got to play his part in a 1–0 win over their local rivals, Birmingham City.

'The city is ours!' Jack posted on social media, with a photo of the winning Villa team.

It was a happy ending to a disappointing season, both for Jack and his club. His stats were decent – thirty-four games, five goals, five assists – but he knew he could do much better than that, especially in the Championship. He wasn't a kid anymore; it was time for him to start fulfilling his amazing potential. He would need to turn his flashes of brilliance into consistent form if he wanted to become a Premier League player again.

And the same was true when it came to his international career. Although he was named in the England squad for the European Under-21 Championships that summer, he didn't play a single minute. In football, everything could change so fast, and wonderkids could be quickly forgotten. One minute, Jack had been the Premier League's next big star, and now, a second season in the Championship beckoned.

CHAPTER 16

SECOND SEASON LUCKY?

With the new Championship season just one week away, Aston Villa took on Watford in a tribute match for their former manager, Graham Taylor. For the players, it was supposed to be a friendly warm-up game, but for Jack, it ended in serious injury. After a brilliant first twenty-five minutes, he went up for a header against Tom Cleverley and fell in a heap on the floor.

'Arghhhhhh!' he cried out in agony, clutching his side.

It didn't look like a dangerous challenge, and so the game carried on. Jack, however, stayed down on the edge of the Watford box, and eventually play stopped so that the physio could come on.

'What's happened to Grealish?' everyone wondered.

The answer was that as they battled for the ball, Cleverley had accidentally kicked Jack in the kidney, and the pain was excruciating, like nothing he had ever felt before. The Villa medical staff helped him off the pitch and took him straight to hospital, where the news wasn't good.

'I'm afraid you've split your kidney in two places,' the doctor explained in a hurry. 'There's a lot of internal bleeding, so you're going to need an operation straight away.'

As the nurses rushed him away to a different hospital, Jack lay there, feeling shocked and scared. Woah, what was going on? He was about to have serious surgery! What if he didn't fully recover and could never play professional football again?

Fortunately, the surgery went well, but the road to recovery was long and frustrating. The one positive was that Jack had lots of time to think about football – how much he loved the game, what he wanted to achieve, and how it had nearly been taken away from him.

'I've really got to start making the most of my talent,' he decided.

For the next few months, Jack worked harder than he'd ever worked before – first in the gym and then on the training field. He was so determined to come back better than ever, and at last, in early November, he achieved his aim.

Coming on for Number Six, Glenn Whelan...
Number Ten, Jaaaaack GREALISH!!!

Hurraaaaaaaaaaaaaaaaaaaaaaaay!

After over three months out, it was amazing to hear such a warm welcome home at Villa Park. As he high-fived Glenn on the touchline, Jack might not have looked like a different person, other than the new number on his back, but he certainly felt like one – stronger, fitter, and much more focused.

'It's great to have you back!' Steve Bruce said with a smile.

Despite his best efforts, Jack wasn't able to make an instant impact for his team, but the atmosphere at Villa had changed completely, from angry and negative to happy and positive. Now, he had a manager who believed in him, and also an inspirational captain who led by example.

When Jack had first heard that John Terry was joining Villa, he couldn't believe it. John Terry, Chelsea's five-time Premier League champion and Champions League winner?! It sounded too good to be true, but no, there he was, arriving at the training ground, and Jack made it his mission to learn as much as he could from the great man. John was so professional in everything he did – the healthy eating, the extra gym sessions after training, the ice baths and massages for recovery. He was not only the first player to arrive every morning, but also the last to leave.

'So, that's what it takes to be so successful!' Jack realised, and game by game, he got better and better. He grabbed his first assist against Leeds United, then another against Bristol City, and then an absolute beauty against Barnsley...

'You genius!' Conor Hourihane cheered, pointing at Jack, after he had danced through the defence and picked him out with a perfect pass.

Then finally, Jack's first goal of the season occurred,

in the game against Burton Albion. He started the move in his own half and then finished it off with a superb volley into the bottom corner.

Goooooooooooooooooooooaaaaaaaaaaaaaaaaalllllllllllllll lllllllllllll!!!!!!!!!!!!!!!!!!!!!

At last! With his fists clenched, Jack slid towards the Villa fans on his knees and threw his arms up in the air. What a feeling! Not only was he producing moments of magic again, but more importantly, he was also helping his team to win football matches. That victory kept Villa in fourth place, just one point behind Derby County who were in joint second place.

'Come on, Premier League here we come!' Jack urged his teammates on.

After missing so much of the season, he was making the most of every match. With a beautiful assist for Albert Adomah, Jack led Villa past Birmingham in the Second City Derby, and then, with a sensational volley of his own, he helped them beat their promotion rivals, Cardiff City.

'Get in!' he cried out as his teammates congratulated him.

Unfortunately, it was Cardiff who claimed second place in the end, but Villa held on to finish fourth. All was not lost; they still had a chance to reach the Premier League through the Championship Play-offs, and Jack was determined to get them there. In the semi-finals against Middlesbrough, his clever corner-kick set up Mile Jedinak to score, and that goal was enough to take them through to the final.

'Yes Jacky, another big game from you!' John Terry shouted, putting his arm around his shoulder as they walked down the tunnel together.

Jack and his team were heading back to Wembley! He hadn't played there since Villa's FA Cup final thrashing at the hands of Arsenal in 2015, and he was hoping for a more enjoyable experience this time. The first goal of the 2018 Championship Play-off final, however, went to Fulham. It was their Number 10, Tom Cairney, who scored it, after a smart run and finish past Sam Johnstone.

What could Villa's Number 10 do to respond? All eyes were on Jack; he was expected to be the bright spark for his team. Just before half-time, he blazed a shot over the bar, and then in the second half, he really came alive. He was in the zone where nothing could stop him, not even nasty kicks and tackles. Suddenly, he was at the centre of everything: passing, crossing, and of course, dribbling. From the halfway line, Jack carried the ball all the way into the Fulham box, past one defender, then another, then another...

'SHOOT!' the Villa fans screamed, jumping to their feet, but at the end of his brilliant solo run, Jack couldn't quite beat the keeper.

'Noooooooooooo!' he groaned with his hands on his head. So nearly an incredible equaliser!

For Villa, it just wasn't meant to be. Even when Denis Odoi was sent off for a bad foul on Jack, they couldn't grab the goal they needed. Jack did his best to create one last big chance, but where was the support from his fellow attackers? He couldn't lead them to the Premier League on his own!

When the final whistle blew, Jack crouched down on the halfway line in disappointment and despair. He had worked so hard to come back from injury and improve as a player and a professional, but for now, there was no fairytale ending to the story. Villa had come so close to promotion, but instead, they merely had another long season in the Championship to look forward to.

CHAPTER 17

CAPTAIN COMEBACK!

Once the disappointment of losing the Championship Play-off final had faded a little, Jack was able to look back proudly at his progress. After an awful start to the season, he had come back brilliantly and taken his game to a higher level. So, what next?

Jack's dream was still to lead his boyhood club back to the top division, but after two attempts, was it maybe time to move on? He had top Premier League clubs chasing him again, and that was where he needed to be playing if he wanted to reach the England senior squad. And, this time, Villa desperately needed the money. After missing out on promotion, the situation was so bad that they were even willing to sell their young superstar for £20 million. Wow, what a bargain!

The Tottenham chairman, Daniel Levy, however, believed he could buy Jack for an even lower price, and so he tried to negotiate. But the transfer discussions went on for so long that eventually, Villa found rich new owners, and suddenly, the asking price doubled to £40 million! On Deadline Day, Tottenham made a final bid of £25 million, but Villa said no. Their star player was no longer for sale.

'What? No, they said I could leave!' Jack couldn't believe it. He had been all ready to return to the Premier League and he had even waved goodbye to the Villa fans after their 3–1 win at Hull City. But there was nothing he could do about it now, so he switched his attention back to getting Villa promoted again.

'Let's get to work. #AVFC,' he posted on social media.

Although John and Gabby had both stopped playing over the summer, there were two new signings that Jack was particularly excited about: a Scottish central

midfielder called John McGinn, and the Chelsea
striker Tammy Abraham.

'Great to have you here, bro!' he welcomed
his England Under-21 teammate to the club. The
previous year, Tammy had scored twenty-three goals
for Bristol City, and now, with Jack setting him up,
surely he would score even more!

That was the plan, but it took a little while for
everything to click together. After ten games, Villa
were way down in fifteenth place with only three
wins. Not good enough! The new owners expected
more, and so they sacked Bruce and replaced him
with the Brentford manager, Dean Smith.

Jack was sorry to see Bruce go, but he got on
brilliantly with Smith straight away. They were two
Brummies and lifelong Villa fans with the same aim:
to lead the club back up to the Premier League where
they belonged.

'And you're the superstar that's going to get us
there,' Smith told Jack.

With his new manager's full support, Jack was soon
back to his magical, match-winning best with goals

against Bolton and Birmingham and assists against Nottingham Forest and West Brom. But just as Villa started to climb up the table, disaster struck again. With his dribbling skills, Jack was used to dealing with heavy tackles from defenders; he was the Championship's most-fouled player after all. But away at local rivals West Brom, he received a few too many kicks and had to hobble off the field early.

'It's my shin,' Jack told his manager with a sad shake of the head. 'Arghhh, the pain's getting worse.'

Smith rested his star player for the next match against Stoke City, but after another medical scan, Jack's spell on the sidelines turned into weeks and then months: December, January, February…

'When will Grealish be fit again?' the fans and journalists were desperate to know. 'We need him back!'

Without their star player, Villa were struggling in mid-table.

'Soon,' Smith replied hopefully.

Just like with his kidney injury the previous season, Jack worked tirelessly on his comeback.

And after weeks of gruelling sessions with the club's fitness coach, Oli Stevenson, he could really feel the difference. He had always had big, powerful legs, but now he had a much stronger upper body too.

'Try knocking me off the ball now, Chezzie!' Jack joked with Villa's centre-back, James Chester, when he returned to first team training.

Now, the next step was playing matches again. Jack couldn't wait; he had missed football so much. At last, in early March, the Villa medical staff agreed that he was ready to return to action. So, would the manager start him off slowly with a few minutes as a sub? No way! Not only did Smith put Jack straight back into the starting line-up against Derby County, but he also handed him the armband.

Jack was the new Villa captain – another of his childhood dreams was about to come true! Leading his team out at Villa Park for the first time was one of the proudest moments of his life, and he was determined to live up to his new role on the pitch.

In the ninth minute, Jack collected the ball in midfield, turned beautifully and then picked out

Tammy with a perfect long pass over the Derby defence. He squared it to Conor Hourihane for an easy finish, but really the goal was all about the vision of the new Villa captain. *1–0!*

'Welcome back, bro!' Tammy shouted as the team celebrated together.

As half-time approached, Villa were 3–0 up, with one last corner before the break. The big centre-backs were waiting in the middle, but instead, Glenn floated the ball out towards Jack on the edge of the penalty area. Woah, was Jack really going to – yes, he watched it carefully onto his right boot and struck it sweetly on the volley. The technique was breathtaking, and the ball swerved past the keeper and into the corner before he could even move. *4–0!*

Gooooooooooooooooooooaaaaaaaaaaaaaaaaaallllllllllllll llllllllllllll!!!!!!!!!!!!!!!!!!!!

What a sensational strike – Villa's magician was back with a BANG! Jack was so happy to be home again, and next up was the Second City Derby against Birmingham!

Away at St Andrew's, the atmosphere was always

intense, but on this occasion, the violence made its
way onto the pitch. In the fifth minute, a Birmingham
player was booked for a terrible tackle on Jack, and
five minutes later, an angry supporter ran onto the
field and attacked Jack ferociously.

'Argghhh!' Jack cried out in shock as he collapsed
to the grass. What was going on?

In his younger days, he might have reacted badly
and fought back with his fists, but things were
different now that Jack was Villa captain. He had to
behave responsibly, and so he kept calm and carried
on playing. He knew that the right way to react was
to go and win the match for Villa.

And that's exactly what he did. Midway through
the second half, Jack got the ball and dribbled into the
Birmingham box, daring a defender to come and foul
him. When no-one did, he went for goal, firing a low
shot into the bottom corner. *1–0!*

*Goooooooooooooooooooooaaaaaaaaaaaaaaaalllllllllllllll
llllllllllll!!!!!!!!!!!!!!!!!!!!*

What a hero! With his arms flying all over the
place, Jack jumped over the advertising boards and

into the arms of the Villa fans.

> *Super, Super Jack,*
> *Super, Super Jack,*
> *Super, Super Jack,*
> *Super Jacky Grealish!*

When the final whistle blew thirty minutes later, Jack punched the air with passion. He had done it – he had scored the winner in the Second City Derby! He had dreamed of this moment so many times as a boy, and now aged twenty-three, he had finally achieved it. And as the Villa captain too! So what if he'd been hit by a Birmingham fan?

'It's the best day of my life,' Jack said with a big smile for the TV cameras.

What next? With their incredible captain back, Villa were full of confidence and flying. From thirteenth place, they jumped to ninth, then eighth, then seventh... could they really make the play-offs again? Yes! With ten wins in a row, they finished the season in fifth place. Unbelievable!

'But we're not done yet, boys,' Jack told his teammates. 'We're going back to Wembley, and this time, we're going to win!'

Hurraaaaaaaaay!

At the end of two tight games, Villa held their nerve to beat West Brom on penalties and book their place in the Play-off Final against Derby. Could Jack produce another moment of magic like his wonderstrike earlier in the season? His club was counting on him…

But Villa weren't such a one-man team anymore. Yes Jack was still their superstar and their leader, but they now had quality players all over the pitch, like:

Anwar El Ghazi, who headed home just before half-time – *1–0!*

And Jack's new best mate, John McGinn, who scored the second – *2–0!*

With ten minutes to go, Derby pulled one goal back, but it wasn't enough. Villa were the winners and it was promotion time at last! With his arms out wide, Jack ran towards the fans and then slid on his knees in front of them.

Yessssssssssssssssssssss!

Since his comeback from injury, Villa had turned their season around completely – from thirteenth place in March to Play-off Champions in May!

WE ARE GOING UP, SAY WE ARE GOING UP!

Later on, after lifting the trophy, Jack walked around Wembley holding one handle, while his manager, Dean Smith, held the other. Together, the two Brummies and lifelong Villa fans had achieved their aim: to lead the club back up to the Premier League where they belonged.

CHAPTER 18

A PREMIER LEAGUE PLAYER AGAIN!

Now that he had helped get Villa promoted, Jack had a point to prove in the Premier League. He still held the embarrassing record for the worst-ever season – sixteen games, sixteen defeats. Surely, he would be more successful second time around?

'Of course, I will,' Jack declared confidently, but behind the scenes, he was working hard to get ready for life in the Premier League. Even when he went on holiday with his family, he still got up early each morning to train.

'Skipper's been doing this every day in Dubai preparing for preseason,' Jack's brother posted on social media with a short video of his fitness session.

After three challenging years in the Championship, Jack couldn't wait to step up and test himself at the highest level against top defenders like Liverpool's Virgil van Dijk, and against world-class playmakers like Manchester City's Kevin De Bruyne.

Villa were one of the favourites to go down and their 2019–20 season started badly – they lost their first two games – but on 23 August against Everton, Jack finally finished back on the winning team in a Premier League match. Hurray!

It was a huge relief to end his horrible run, but Jack was soon worrying about his own performances. Was he doing enough to help his team? Villa were relying on him to be their creative spark, and that didn't just mean nice touches and turns; it meant proper end product – goals and assists. He was doing lots of dribbling and winning lots of free kicks, but after five games, Jack only had one assist: a simple pass to set up a screamer from Douglas Luiz against Bournemouth.

'Hey, don't worry about that yet,' Dean Smith reassured his captain. 'You're at your best when you're having fun on the football pitch. Don't put so much pressure on yourself straight away. Just enjoy playing in the Premier League, and the goals will come, I promise.'

As usual, his manager was right. With Villa 2–0 up and cruising to victory away at Norwich City, Jack got on the ball and did what he did best – dribble! When he reached the edge of the area, he passed right to Anwar, who passed it back for the one-two.

'SHOOT!' the Villa fans urged, and with his weaker left foot, Jack guided the ball beautifully into the bottom corner. *3–0!*

Goooooooooooooooooooaaaaaaaaaaaaaaaaalllllllllllllll lllllllllll!!!!!!!!!!!!!!!!!!!

At last! Four years after his Premier League goal, Jack finally had his second, and his third arrived in the very next match against Brighton. It wasn't one of his usual wonderstrikes, though; instead, he slid the ball in from five yards out like an old-school striker. *1–1!*

'Come on, let's win this now!' Jack urged his teammates on.

After that, Villa attacked and attacked, looking for a second goal, but it seemed like they'd run out of time. With Jack on the pitch and on the ball, however, there was always a chance. With just seconds to go, he controlled a pass on the left wing and dribbled fearlessly at the Brighton defence. As he entered the box, two players blocked his path, but Jack managed to slip the ball through to Matt Targett, who fired a shot into the far corner. *2–1!*

Villa Park – not just the supporters in the stands but also the players on the pitch – went absolutely wild for that last-minute winner. What a massive moment it was in their struggle to stay in the Premier League! And at the centre of the big team huddle was Jack, the hero who had saved the day with a goal and a game-winning assist.

'A captain's performance,' was how his manager described it, and there were lots more of those to come.

Away at Old Trafford, it was two Villa attackers versus four Manchester United defenders when Jack got the ball on the left side of the box. It didn't look like a particularly dangerous position, but with four quick taps and a body swerve, Jack glided straight past

Andreas Pereira and then curled a shot over David De Gea and into the top corner. *1–0!*

Goooooooooooooooooooaaaaaaaaaaaaaaaaalllllllllllll llllllllllll!!!!!!!!!!!!!!!!!!!!

It was another sensational strike, and against one of the best teams in the world, but Jack jogged away to celebrate as if it was nothing special.

'Mate, that was magic!' Conor cheered in disbelief.

In the end, the match finished 2–2, and Villa had another precious point to add to their total.

15 points...

'Well done, lads,' Jack told his teammates. 'Twenty-five more and we're definitely staying up!'

Sometimes, his goals and assists weren't enough to change games, like at home against Leicester or away at Southampton. But the more Jack scored, the more his confidence grew, and the better he became. He was finally fulfilling his amazing potential as one of the Premier League's leading playmakers!

After four defeats in a row in December, however, Villa slipped down into the relegation zone. Uh oh, they really needed a win at home against Norwich,

but they got it, thanks to Jack. With his team in
trouble, he danced his way into the box and then
cleverly poked the ball across to Conor. *1–0!*

Come onnnnnnnnnnnnnn!

...18 points...

Conor had scored the crucial goal, but he ran
straight over to celebrate with Jack. What would Villa
do without their incredible captain? 'Get relegated,'
the answer appeared to be.

Away at Burnley, Jack set up the first goal for
Wesley Moraes and then scored the second himself,
smashing a shot into the top corner with power and
accuracy.

'Yesssssss!' Jack yelled, punching the air. It was
his sixth Premier League goal of the season, and most
importantly, it meant three more precious points for
Villa.

...21 points...

Away at Brighton, they were 1–0 down with
twenty minutes to go, but Jack rescued a point with
a fantastic left-foot strike.

...22 points...

Watford went 1–0 up at Villa Park, but back the home team battled, led by their brilliant captain. Douglas Luiz grabbed the equaliser, and then Ezri Konsa scored the winner in the very last minute.

…25 points!

Jack was so proud of his teammates and the spirit they were showing. 'We're staying up, lads. I'm sure of it!' he urged them on.

But first, Villa were through to the EFL Cup semi-finals, where they faced Leicester City. They were one win away from another trip to Wembley, and it was all set to be an exciting battle between two of the Premier League's top new playmakers: Jack Grealish and James Maddison. They had been good friends for years, but which would lead their team to the final?

The first chance fell to James. He dribbled into the Villa box and fired a low shot towards the bottom corner, but Ørjan Nyland got down to push it past the post.

'Ooooooh!' James gasped with his hands on his head. Nearly!

A few minutes later, it was Jack's turn to attack

at the other end. As he entered the Leicester box,
Ricardo Pereira and Çağlar Söyüncü were marking
him closely, so Jack slowed down to wait for Matt to
catch up and then found him with a lovely flick pass.
1–0!

It was advantage Villa and advantage Jack, but the
battle was only just getting started. James's curling
shot was blocked by Marvelous Nakamba, then Jack's
teasing cross flew just inches past Mbwana Ally
Samatta's outstretched leg. So close! It was his turn to
stand there with his hands on his head. How had they
not scored a second goal there?

It looked like Villa would regret that miss when
James set up Harvey Barnes, who crossed to Kelechi
Iheanacho. *1–1!* But Jack still believed and so did his
teammates. With seconds to go before extra-time,
Ahmed Elmohamady curled in a high ball towards
Trézéguet at the back post, and he finished in style.
2–1 to Villa!

'Get in!' Jack yelled as he raced across the pitch.
'We're going to Wembley!'

Villa's opponents in the EFL Cup final would be

Manchester City, who had won the trophy for the last two years in a row. In the Premier League that season, City had already thrashed them twice – 3–0 away and then 6–1 at home. Were Villa heading for another humiliating defeat like against Arsenal in 2015?

'No, we've got to believe we can beat them!' Jack declared with determination. He was desperate to win a trophy for his club.

With thirty minutes played, however, it looked like City had won the trophy already. They were 2–0 up, thanks to goals from Sergio Agüero and Rodri.

'Noooooooo!' Jack groaned, throwing his head back in frustration. Too easy!

But instead of giving up, the Villa captain got on the ball and pushed his team forward on the attack with quick, clever passes. And it worked. Just before half-time, Ally Samatta powered a diving header past Claudio Bravo. *2–1!*

'Yes, game on!' Jack roared as the players ran back for the restart.

Could Villa now go on and get an equaliser? They gave it absolutely everything in the second half, but in the end, it wasn't quite enough. Runners-up again! At the final whistle, Jack lay flat on the grass with his head in his hands, exhausted and emotional. Another Wembley disappointment was so hard to take.

Jack and his teammates couldn't dwell on that EFL Cup final defeat for long, however, because they had other problems to worry about. Back in the Premier League, the season was about to be suspended due to COVID-19, just as Villa were placed second from bottom. Were they destined to go back down, or could they somehow stay up? It felt like only one man could save them...

CHAPTER 19

FROM VILLAIN TO ENGLAND HERO

How long would the coronavirus pandemic last? And how long would it be before the Premier League season could restart? Jack missed playing football so much! He did his best to keep himself busy by doing fitness work at home and playing *Fortnite*, but it wasn't the same as going training with his teammates.

'I'd really love a kickabout right now!' he complained on a call with John.

By the end of March 2020, Jack was so bored of being stuck indoors that unfortunately he let his football focus slip. One night, he decided to break the lockdown rules and go to a friend's house for a party, and he ended up crashing his car. The next day, his face was all over the newspapers, with headlines like:

'BRAINLESS'

and

'COVIDIOT'

Uh-oh, Jack was in big trouble. What a stupid mistake! He felt awful about letting everyone down – his manager, his teammates, the club, the NHS, and all of the kids who looked up to him as a role model. He had to do his best to make things right. So after posting a public apology on social media, he concentrated all of his attention on keeping Villa in the Premier League.

In late May, Jack was able to start training with his teammates again at last. 'Buzzing to be back,' he tweeted, and a week later, there was more good news. It was official; the Premier League season would be restarting on 17 June. Hurray!

At first, Jack found it really weird playing football in empty, quiet stadiums. He really missed the cheers from the crowd, but hey, it was still much better than not playing football at all. Plus, with ten games to go, Villa's priority wasn't to entertain; it was to stay in the

Premier League.

'Let's do this!' Jack clapped and cheered as he led his team out against Sheffield United.

In their first six matches back, however, Villa only managed to pick up two points out of a possible eighteen. What a disaster! The team had problems at both ends of the pitch – the defence was conceding too many goals, and the strikers were hardly scoring at all.

'Someone get your head on that!' Jack moaned, growing more and more frustrated. He was creating chance after chance, but if no-one finished them off, then what could he do? The only good news was that Watford and Bournemouth were struggling to win games too.

'Come on, we can still stay up this season!' Smith tried to spur his players on before the first of what felt like four big cup finals:

1) Aston Villa 2 Crystal Palace 0
30 points – their chances of Premier League survival were still alive, thanks to two goals from Trezeguet!

2) Everton 1 Aston Villa 1

31 points – a decent draw away at Goodison Park.

3) Aston Villa 1 Arsenal 0

34 points – and they were out of the relegation zone for the first time since February! The winner arrived midway through the first half, through Trezeguet again, and after that, it was all about defending for Villa. Everyone was back helping out, even Jack. Late in the second half, he intercepted a pass just outside his own penalty area and pushed his team up the pitch to relieve the pressure. First, he used his strength to escape from Eddie Nketiah, and then his skill to skip past Dani Ceballos.

'Go on, Grealish!' the Villa supporters shouted excitedly at their TV screens.

After crossing the halfway line, Jack looked up and slipped a perfect pass through to Keinan Davis. The young striker was in, with just the keeper to beat... but his shot rolled just wide of the post.

'Nooooooo!' Jack groaned. Would that prove to be a very important miss? No, Aston Villa stayed strong and held on for the win, which meant that with one game to go, the bottom of the Premier League table looked like this:

17 Aston Villa	34 points
18 Watford	34 points
19 Bournemouth	31 points
20 Norwich City	21 points

What drama for the final day of the season! At half-time, Watford were losing 2–1 away at Arsenal…

'Yesss!'

…Bournemouth were winning 2–1 away at Everton…

'Nooo!'

…And Villa? They were drawing 0–0 at West Ham. As things stood, that result would be enough to keep them up, but they couldn't rely on Watford losing.

'We've got to win ourselves!' Jack told his teammates.

After fourteen Premier League games without a goal or assist, plus his bad behaviour during lockdown, it was really time for Jack to step up and shine for Villa. Early in the second half, Jack danced his way into the

West Ham box, but his shot was saved. He just had to keep on trying…

With less than ten minutes to go, the score was still 0–0, but Jack was still full of belief. As the pass from John arrived, two defenders surrounded him and forced him wide on his weaker foot, but that didn't bother Jack. With a swing of his left leg, he sent a shot dipping and swerving past the West Ham keeper. *1–0!*

Goooooooooooooooooooooaaaaaaaaaaaaaaaallllllllllllllllll llllllllllllll!!!!!!!!!!!!!!!!!!!!!

Thanks to another moment of magic, Jack was the Villa hero! It was his eighth goal of the season, and his most important by far. 'Come onnnnnnn!' he cried out as he spun away to celebrate. But with no Villa supporters there in the stadium, he sprinted over to the bench to hug the subs and coaching staff instead.

Yesssssssssssssssssssss!

That should have been Premier League safety secured for Villa, but a minute later, West Ham were on the attack and Andriy Yarmolenko's shot deflected off Jack's boot and looped up over Pepe Reina's head. *1–1!*

Noooooooooooooooooo!

Jack and his teammates couldn't believe what had just happened, but they had to keep their concentration until the final whistle blew. Right, now to check on the other results...

The Villa players and coaches stood together in a huddle on the pitch, waiting for the final score at Arsenal. Watford had pulled another goal back to make it 3–2, but could they grab a last-gasp equaliser? No!

'Lads, we're staying up!' Smith shouted to start the Villa celebrations.

YESSSSSSSSSSSSSSSSSSS!

With his manager's arm around his shoulder, Jack bounced up and down with joy and relief. What a day and what a season! It had taken one last push from the captain, but he had done it. Jack had achieved his aim of keeping his club in the Premier League!

And his summer was about to get even better. In late August, Marcus Rashford had to pull out of England's squad for the UEFA Nations League due to an ankle injury, and who did Gareth Southgate select to replace him? Jack!

'A dream come true to receive my first senior call up,' he tweeted proudly.

What an honour – at last, all of his hard work had paid off! In that moment, Jack felt like everything had been worth it: saying no to Ireland, staying loyal to Aston Villa, fighting his way up from the Championship to the Premier League, the ups and the downs, the lessons learned. It was all part of the amazing journey that had led him to this: Jack Grealish, England senior international.

'Let's go!'

Jack couldn't wait to join up with the squad and start training with world-class superstars like Harry Kane and Raheem Sterling, as well as old friends like Tammy Abraham and his Villa teammate, Tyrone Mings. But most of all, he couldn't wait to make his England debut.

After watching from the bench as they beat Iceland 1–0, Jack's big moment finally arrived in the seventy-sixth minute against Denmark. With the score at 0–0, Southgate sent him on to try and create a winning goal for the team.

'Cheers, boss!' he said with a big smile, showing no signs of fear. Nothing fazed him, not even international football. So, when the ball arrived, Jack just did what he did best at Villa: dribble!

On the left wing, he weaved his way towards the Denmark box, past one player, and then in between two more, until eventually a fourth defender came across to make the tackle.

'Unlucky, Jack!'

And then on the right wing, he used his skill and stepovers to win a corner for his team.

'Great work, Jack!'

Sadly, there was to be no winning goal for England, but for Jack, it was a pretty impressive first performance during just fifteen minutes on the pitch.

'He is a different type of player to any that we have,' Southgate told the media after the match.

So did that mean Jack had done enough to earn a second cap soon? He would just have to wait and see.

CHAPTER 20

A SPECIAL KIND OF SUPERSTAR

Just days after making his England debut, Jack sat down to sign a big new five-year contract at Aston Villa.

'My city, my club, my home,' he posted on social media alongside happy pictures of him with his dog.

Despite interest from Manchester United and Arsenal, Jack had decided to stay at Villa Park for at least another season. And after that? Well, if one of the top six teams really wanted to sign him, they would have to pay the new release clause in his contract – £100 million!

Would a club really be willing to pay £100 million for an English player? Well, Jack was a special kind of superstar now, as he soon showed against the new Premier League champions.

With two wins out of two, Villa had made a flying start to the new 2020–21 season and so they approached the game against Liverpool with excitement, not fear. It was a chance for them to test themselves against the best team in the country.

'Let's show them we're a different side this year!' cried captain Jack, and he led by example. In the fourth minute, he raced into the penalty area to collect a poor pass from the Liverpool keeper, and then squared the ball to Villa's new striker, Ollie Watkins. *1–0!*

'Thanks, mate!' Ollie cheered, giving Jack a high-five.

Villa were off to the perfect start, and their captain was putting on a real midfield masterclass. Twenty minutes later, Jack carried the ball forward over the halfway line and then at the perfect moment, he poked a pass through to Ollie, who fired a shot into the top corner. *2–0!*

'What a finish!' Jack called out as he jumped into

Ollie's arms. Their partnership was already looking really promising.

When Liverpool pulled a goal back, Villa didn't drop deep and defend. No, they carried on attacking with confidence.

John McGinn's volley deflected in off van Dijk. *3–1!*

Ollie completed his hat-trick with a header. *4–1!*

Villa were on fire, and they didn't slow down in the second half. Ollie won the ball back and played it to Ross Barkley, who played a double one-two with Jack before finding the net. *5–1!*

'Yes mate, what a debut, eh?' Jack shouted as he gave his new teammate a big hug.

Villa were winning 5–1 and their captain hadn't even scored! Yet. But after setting up three goals for his teammates, Jack was still desperate to grab at least one goal of his own.

'Yes, mate – pass it!' he yelled out as Ollie burst through the middle.

When the ball arrived, Jack dribbled straight at Trent Alexander-Arnold, daring him to try and tackle him. He didn't, so with a drop of the shoulder, Jack decided to cut inside and shoot instead. BANG! The ball thundered into Fabinho's body and then into the bottom corner. *6–2!*

Goooooooooooooooooooaaaaaaaaaaaaaaaaalllllllllllllll lllllllllll!!!!!!!!!!!!!!!!!

'Get in!' He was on the scoresheet at last, but Jack could do better than a dodgy, deflected goal. So, ten minutes later, he raced onto a super pass from John and coolly fooled the keeper. *7–2!*

Jack celebrated with a knee slide and a cheeky smile. What a win against the Premier League Champions, and what a captain's performance! Two goals and three assists – those were superstar stats, and after the match, the Liverpool manager Jürgen Klopp was full of praise for him:

'Jack Grealish, what a footballer!'

Everyone now knew what he was capable of, but could Jack keep his fantastic form going and shine consistently every week? Yes, of course he could! Jack's younger days of just dribbling for fun were over; as Villa captain, he was all about winning games for his team now. So, whether it was a training session or a proper Premier League match, Jack was fully focused on getting as many goals and assists as he possibly could.

A cross for Tyrone and then a long-range swerver against Southampton,

A run from his own half to set up Ollie against Arsenal,

A stunning strike against West Ham,

A brilliant ball to Bertrand Traoré against Manchester United,

And then another against Newcastle United...

Super, Super Jack,
Super, Super Jack,
Super, Super Jack,
Super Jacky Grealish!

Six goals, twelve assists, and over seventy chances created – what a superstar season he was having! Jack was nominated for Premier League Player of the Month in October, November and January. And with their captain leading the way, Villa were a team on the rise. Instead of fighting relegation like last year, now they were flying high in the top half of the table.

But then, just as the fans began to dream of a return to European football, their worst fears came true. In mid-February 2021, Jack injured his shin again. Oh no, not their incredible captain! How would Villa cope without him? 'Not very well' was the answer. Jack watched from the sidelines as they won only one of their next six league matches.

'Please boss, I'm ready to play again!' Jack begged Dean Smith from the moment he was fit enough to return to training. His team needed him, and his manager knew it. But as Jack prepared for his comeback game against Liverpool, he suffered an injury setback. Noooooooooo, he was facing even more weeks without football!

'Doing everything to be back fitter and stronger than ever,' Jack explained to his disappointed fans.

Eventually, after missing twelve matches, he finally made his comeback as a second-half sub against Everton. Although there were still no supporters in the stands at Villa Park, it was amazing to be out there on the pitch again. Playing football for his boyhood club really was the best feeling in the world. A week later, Jack returned to the starting line-up and ended the season in style by leading his team to victories over Tottenham and Chelsea. What a captain, what a special kind of superstar!

The timing was perfect – Jack was back to his match-winning best, and Euro 2020 was only weeks away.

CHAPTER 21

EURO 2020:
BEST SUMMER EVER!

Since making his senior England debut against Denmark, Jack had earned four more caps for his country:

Against Wales, where his man-of-the-match performance included an assist for Dominic Calvert-Lewin,

Against his old nation Ireland, where he set up Jadon Sancho to score,

Against Belgium, where he had 'an absolutely outstanding game' according to Southgate, despite England's defeat,

And against Iceland, where he was excellent again.

So, with those superb displays, plus his fantastic Premier League form, had Jack done enough to make the squad for Euro 2020? He really hoped so, but England had so many amazing attackers now: Harry Kane, Raheem Sterling, Marcus Rashford, Phil Foden, Bukayo Saka, Mason Greenwood, Jesse Lingard, James Maddison, Dominic, Jadon, Ollie…There was no way that Southgate could select them all!

Jack, however, offered something different from the others: magic. With the ball at his feet, he was capable of creating something out of nothing, and that was a very useful talent to have in a tournament squad…

On 1 June, the final list of twenty-six names were announced at the end of a special new England song called 'The Call-Up', written by rapper Wretch 32. And in amongst the eight attackers, there was his name:

'JACK GREALISH'

Yessss, it was really happening! From his first experience of Rooney at Euro 2004 all the way through to the 2018 World Cup, Jack had always cheered the team on as an England fan. But this time, he would be there as an actual England player!

'An absolute honour to make the squad for the Euros this summer,' he posted on social media. 'I've always dreamt about playing in a major tournament for my country! Let's make it a summer to remember.'

Now that he had made England's Euro 2020 squad, Jack moved on to his next challenge: making the starting line-up. That wasn't going to be easy, though, because there was only really one spot up for grabs in Southgate's first-choice front-three. It would be Harry, Raheem, and who???

Raheem preferred to play on the left side of the attack, but no problem, Jack was happy to switch sides to the right if that got him into the team. He would do whatever England needed him to do! But even when he was handed the Number 7 shirt and he started both of the warm-up games, Jack didn't let himself get carried away. Whatever happened, he was living his childhood dream, and he was just going to enjoy every moment of Euro 2020.

In England's first match against Croatia, it was Phil who started alongside Harry and Raheem, and Marcus and Dominic who came off the bench. Of course, Jack was disappointed not to play at all, but the squad spirit was strong, and the most important thing was that

England had won 1–0, thanks to a goal from Raheem.

'Great start to the tournament,' Jack tweeted in support of his teammates. He just had to keep working hard in training and hope that his chance would come…

Come on, England – get Grealish on!

Jack's first chance arrived in the sixty-third minute of their next game, against Scotland. It was 0–0 with half an hour to go and the fans were growing restless – could he come on and create some of his match-winning magic? Jack tried his very best to spark England into life, but with Scotland defending deep, there was so little space for him to dribble.

'Arghhhh!' Jack groaned at the final whistle, as his shoulders slumped in frustration. 'That was my big chance and I blew it!'

But no, instead Southgate moved him into the starting line-up for England's final group game against the Czech Republic, in a central attacking midfield role. What an opportunity, and this time, Jack made the most of it. In the twelfth minute, he got the ball on the left side of the box and did what he did best – dribble!

The two Czech defenders knew how dangerous Jack could be if he cut inside on his right foot, so they forced him wide on his weaker side instead. That seemed like a smart plan, but it didn't work because Jack could cross the ball beautifully with his left foot too. CHIP! It was just too high for Bukayo, but Raheem swooped in behind him to head the ball home. 1–0!

'Yesssssss!' Jack cheered, throwing his arms up in the air as he raced over to join his teammates. England were winning, thanks to his first assist at Euro 2020! He was already a fans' favourite, but now, the eyes of the whole football world were on him.

'Grealish has got to start every game,' people were saying all over social media. 'He's such a joy to watch!'

Southgate, however, decided to start Bukayo instead for their Round of 16 clash with Germany. He was a better defender than Jack, but with the game still goalless in the second half, the fans began calling for their favourite player:

Get Grealish on!

With twenty minutes to go, Jack ran onto the pitch and helped change the game almost instantly. Suddenly, England's attacking football flowed. Raheem passed forward to Harry, who passed back to Jack, who passed left to Luke Shaw, who crossed it into the middle for Raheem. *1–0!*

'Come onnnnnnn!' Jack yelled as he chased after his teammates.

When they moved the ball around like that, they made the game look so simple, and ten minutes later, they did it again. This time, Luke passed left to Jack, who got his second assist of the tournament, curling in another lovely left-foot cross for Harry to head home. *2–0!*

> *'It's coming home, it's coming home,*
> *It's coming, FOOTBALL'S COMING HOME!'*

The 40,000 England fans at Wembley were going wild and so were the players on the pitch. They were on their way to the Euro 2020 quarter-finals!

After his super sub performance, Jack had to start

the next game against Ukraine, surely? But no, Southgate went for Jadon instead, and with England winning 4–0 after sixty-five minutes, he stayed on the bench.

Oh well, what about the semi-final against Denmark? Yes, Jack came on in the seventieth minute with the game tied at 1–1, and he got so close to grabbing his third Euro 2020 assist. At the very end of added time, Jack dribbled into the box and calmly picked out Harry with a brilliant pass... but Simon Kjaer threw himself down to make the block.

'Ooooooh!' Jack gasped with his hands on his head, so nearly England's hero in the ninety-sixth minute.

Instead, they won the semi-final in extra-time, after Raheem was fouled in the penalty area. Harry's spot-kick was saved, but he scored the rebound. *2–1!*

'Yessssssssss!' Jack and his teammates cried as they slid towards the corner flag on their knees. For the first time since 1966, England were going through to the final of a major tournament! The celebrations went on long after the final whistle at Wembley, both on the pitch and in the stands.

'It's coming home, it's coming home,
It's coming, FOOTBALL'S COMING HOME!'

'I love this team,' Jack posted later, too buzzing to sleep and so proud to be a part of it. 'What a night at Wembley!'

And the atmosphere at the final was even better – more supporters and more excitement. Because with one more win, England would be Champions of Europe! Jack watched on from the sidelines as his team took an early lead and then Italy fought back. *1–1!*

Get Grealish on!

The game was crying out for a moment of match-winning magic, but Jack stayed on the bench and on came Bukayo instead. At last, in extra-time, Southgate decided to bring Jack on, but by then, it was too late to make a difference before…

Penalties! Jack was desperate to step up and take one for his team, but the England manager had already picked his first five players:

1) Harry Kane… scored!

Yesssssss!

2) Harry Maguire… scored!

Yesssssss!

3) Marcus… hit the post!

Noooooo!

4) Jadon… had his shot saved!

Noooooo!

5) Bukayo… had his shot saved too!

NOOOOO!

Jack's heart sank as he watched from the halfway line, arm-in-arm with his teammates. That was it; it was all over and Italy, not England, were the Euro 2020 winners.

As the Italians celebrated, Jack stood there frozen in a daze of disappointment, giving glum hugs and high-fives to the players who passed by. For the first time in a long time, he was truly lost for words. What was there to say? The England team had done so well to get that far, uniting the nation with their winning smiles, strong principles, and superb performances on the pitch, but it was so heart-wrenching to lose in the final.

Eventually, however, that feeling did fade, and Jack was able to look back fondly at his Euro 2020 experience. He had so many happy memories – fun times with his teammates on and off the training pitch, playing darts and basketball at St George's Park, his assist against the Czech Republic, his game-changing twenty minutes against Germany, the extra-time win over Denmark…

Yes, it really had been the best summer ever, and England's journey was far from over. They had made so much progress already – from losing in the Round of 16 at Euro 2016 to reaching the final at Euro 2020 – but the players believed that there was even more to come. What next – World Cup winners in 2022? That was the plan, and Jack couldn't wait to play his part.

CHAPTER 22

MANCHESTER CITY'S £100-MILLION MAN

By the time Euro 2020 came to an end, the transfer rumours were already flying, linking Jack with all of Europe's top teams:

Manchester United on verge of completing Grealish deal

Manchester City open talks with Aston Villa over Grealish signing

Liverpool target Grealish

Barcelona, Real Madrid join Grealish race

Wow, suddenly Jack was one of the most-wanted superstars in the world! So, what would he decide to do: stay at Aston Villa or sign for a team in the Champions League?

'Look son, if you choose to move on now, after everything you've done for this club, no-one's going to blame you for that,' his dad assured him.

Jack would always be a Villa fan. It had been his home for nineteen years, as he rose from academy star to first team captain. But after leading them back to the Premier League, all the way to an EFL Cup final, and rescuing them from relegation, what more could he achieve at the club?

Plus, with Jack's twenty-sixth birthday approaching, it felt like the perfect time to take on a big new challenge. While he was at the peak of his footballing powers, Jack wanted to play at the very highest level. After taking on Europe's top national teams at Euro 2020, he now wanted to compete against Europe's top clubs too, in the Champions League, and win lots of trophies.

Jack was ready to go, but would one of the big clubs be willing to break the British transfer record and pay his £100-million release clause? Yes – the Premier

League Champions, Manchester City were willing to!

Pep Guardiola had first praised him back in 2019, saying, 'He's a talented player who always creates something. An exceptional player but too expensive for Manchester!' Since then, however, Jack's superstar performances for Villa and England had changed the City manager's mind. He was now desperate to sign him, however much he cost.

Wow, Jack couldn't believe it. Guardiola was one of the best managers in the world, and City were one of the best teams in the world. Their style of football was so beautiful, with lots of flowing passing moves. He would fit in perfectly! Plus, most importantly, City were a club who won trophies. Not only had they just lifted their fifth Premier League title, but they had also reached the Champions League final after an amazing victorious performance over PSG in the semis.

Ah, the Champions League! For years, Jack had sat at home watching the games on TV and wishing that he could be out there experiencing it for himself. Well, if he signed for City, that wish would become a reality! Was he really about to join their squad of superstars? And was he really about to get the chance to work with Kevin De Bruyne, the most perfect footballer in the Premier League? Surrounded by so much talent, Jack was sure to become an even better player.

Once the deal was done, it was time for the most difficult part: saying an emotional farewell to everyone at Aston Villa. 'I love this club with all my heart,' Jack wrote in a message to the fans, 'and I hope you understand my reasons for seeking a new challenge.'

What a challenge it was going to be! Not only was Jack Manchester City's big new summer signing, but he was also Britain's first-ever £100-million player. Thousands of supporters showed up at the Etihad Stadium to welcome him to the club, and many of them were already wearing '10 GREALISH' shirts.

Woah, the pressure was on, but was he nervous about living up to everyone's high expectations? No, not at all; Jack couldn't wait to get started. He had always believed in his own ability, and this was his chance to show it on the biggest stage. What could be more exciting than that?

Although Jack's career with Manchester City began with two defeats, he was still pleased with his own performances, and so was his manager. 'He had an incredible game,' Guardiola said after City lost 1–0 to Tottenham. 'He will be so important for us.'

And it wasn't long before the goals and assists arrived for Manchester City's £100-million man. On his home debut against Norwich, Jack raced into the right place at the right time to deflect Gabriel Jesus's cross into the net.

Goooooooooooooooooooooaaaaaaaaaaaaaaaaalllllllllllllll llllllllllll!!!!!!!!!!!!!!!!!!!!

'Yessssss!' Jack screamed at the sky, throwing his arms out wide and blowing kisses to the crowd. It wasn't one of his usual wonderstrikes, but hey, who cared about that? What mattered was that he was off the mark for Manchester City!

A week later against Arsenal, Jack collected his first assist for his new club. From wide on the left, he attacked the penalty area with confidence, dribbling at the defence, before poking a clever pass through to Gabriel. *3–0!*

Wow, Jack was settling in so well at City! His new teammates loved playing with him, and he was already a fans' favourite, with a chant of his own:

> *He'll take the ball, he'll beat five men,*
> *He's super City's Number 10,*
> *Jack Grealish! Jack Grealish!*

What a start! Soon, however, it was time for Jack's greatest challenge, the one that he'd waited years for. Champions League football? Bring it on!

City's first opponents, RB Leipzig, were a talented team, who had reached the semi-finals in 2020. But on his grand European debut, Jack was just too good for them. Early in the second half, Rúben Dias booted the ball forward and Jack was onto it in a flash. First touch – control, second touch – attack! With speed and skill, Jack dribbled into the box, past one defender, and then curled a shot into the far corner.

Goooooooooooooooooooooaaaaaaaaaaaaaaaallllllllllllll llllllllllll!!!!!!!!!!!!!!!!!!!!

A wonderstrike on his debut – Jack was made

for Champions League football! He slid towards the
corner flag on his knees, with a big smile on his face,
as the City supporters clapped and cheered. It was the
kind of goal that Jack had been scoring since he first
joined the Aston Villa academy, but the difference was
that now, twenty years later, he was doing it at the
very highest level.

The talent and the belief had always been there,
but after years of ups and downs, setbacks and
frustrations, Jack had finally added the focus and
dedication needed to become a true football superstar.

GREALISH
HONOURS

Aston Villa

🏆 NextGen Series: 2012–13

🏆 EFL Championship play-offs: 2019

England U-21

🏆 Toulon Tournament: 2016

Individual

🏆 FAI Under-17 Irish International Player of
the Year: 2012

🏆 FAI Under-21 Irish International Player of
the Year: 2015

🏆 PFA Championship Team of the Year: 2018–19
🏆 Aston Villa Player of the Season: 2019–20

GREALISH

10 **THE FACTS**

NAME: Jack Peter Grealish

DATE OF BIRTH: 10 September 1995

PLACE OF BIRTH: Solihull, Midlands

NATIONALITY: English

BEST FRIEND: John McGinn

CURRENT CLUB: Manchester City

POSITION: LW

THE STATS

Height (cm):	185
Club appearances:	262
Club goals:	45
Club assists:	61
Club trophies:	1
International appearances:	16
International goals:	1
International trophies:	1
Ballon d'Ors:	0

★ ★ ★ **HERO RATING: 86** ★ ★ ★

GREATEST MOMENTS

19 APRIL 2015,
ASTON VILLA 2–1 LIVERPOOL

This was the match where Jack first made a name
for himself. He was only nineteen years old at the
time and playing at Wembley in an FA Cup semi-final
against Steven Gerrard's Liverpool, but none of that
seemed to faze him at all. Jack got on the ball and
played with his usual joy and freedom, helping to set
up both goals to send Villa through to the final.

10 MARCH 2019,
BIRMINGHAM CITY 0–1 ASTON VILLA

Jack described this as 'the best day of my life'. This was his second game back after a serious injury, his second match as Villa captain, and it was also the big Second City Derby. As a kid, Jack had always dreamed of scoring the winner to beat Birmingham and that's exactly what he did, even after being attacked by a fan on the pitch. Three months later, he then led Villa back to the Premier League.

4 OCTOBER 2020,
ASTON VILLA 7–2 LIVERPOOL

After rescuing Villa from relegation, Jack's next step was to become a proper Premier League superstar. In this game against the reigning champions, he put on a midfield masterclass, running the show while grabbing three assists and two goals. Suddenly, everyone was watching Jack, including England manager, Gareth Southgate…

29 JUNE 2021,
ENGLAND 2–0 GERMANY

Jack was already an England fan's favourite at Euro 2020, but this Round of 16 match was when he became a real national hero. He was only on the pitch for twenty minutes, but Jack changed the game and played a key part in both goals. What a super sub performance!

15 SEPTEMBER 2021,
MANCHESTER CITY 6–3 RB LEIPZIG

Following his £100-million move to Manchester City, Jack couldn't wait to start playing Champions League football. In this, his debut in the competition, he showed what a world-class superstar he now was. In the first half, Jack set up Nathan Aké with a brilliant corner, and then in the second, he dribbled in off the left wing to score a wondergoal of his own.

PLAY LIKE YOUR HEROES

THE JACK GREALISH
DRIBBLE AND SCORE

STEP 1: First things first, you're going to need a bit of space to show off your skills. Drop deep, go wide, move inside – keep going until you find your freedom.

STEP 2: Next, you're going to need the ball! Call for it and when it comes, make sure your first touch is phenomenal.

STEP 3: After one touch to control, it's time to attack! Dribble forward, towards the box, at full speed and with total confidence.

STEP 4: With stuttering steps, dare the defenders to come and tackle you if they can. As they approach, twist and turn, showing that you could go either way if you wanted to.

STEP 5: If they push you wide onto your weaker left foot, try to pick out a teammate with a cross or a pass.

STEP 6: But if you can, drop your shoulder and cut inside onto your stronger right foot. Now, SHOOT! Aim for the top corner with power and plenty of swerve.

STEP 7: GOAL! Celebrate like the superstar you are, with a smile and a knee slide.

TEST YOUR KNOWLEDGE

QUESTIONS

1. What trophy did Jack's great-great grandfather Billy Garraty win with Aston Villa in 1905?

2. Who scored a hat-trick when Jack went to watch his first-ever Aston Villa match?

3. Who was Jack's favourite player at Euro 2004, his first tournament as an England fan?

4. Which other sport did Jack play between the ages of 10 and 14?

5. Which legendary footballer first inspired Jack to wear his socks down low?